The Smart Chick's Guide to Career Happiness:
Discover Your Dream Work

Carol Maloney-Scott

The Smart Chick's Guide to Career Happiness

Copyright Carol Maloney-Scott 2020

All rights reserved. This book or any portion thereof may not be reproduced or used in any manner whatsoever without the express written permission of the publisher except for the use of brief quotations in a book review. For permission requests, please contact the publisher.

Formatting by Wild Seas Formatting (http://www.WildSeasFormatting.com)

http://carolmaloneyscott.com

For

All the Smart Chicks who doubt their GREATNESS on the path to Career Happiness

Let's do this!!!

Foreword

There is nothing I hate more than reading a big, long, drawn out tale about how the author had a terrible life and overcame all the obstacles, and now they stand before you, the triumphant expert!

Well, there are actually things I hate A LOT more, but as you will learn, I am rather dramatic when making a point.

Even though I am not a fan of vanity or self-indulgence, I hope you will view my personal sharing in the spirit it is intended – to help you to see that we all make mistakes (sometimes whopper doozies!) and it's never too late to manifest into reality the career of your dreams.

So, I *am* going to share my story – but instead of a long autobiography that delays your immersion into the meat of this guide, I am going to sprinkle my saga throughout this book, where sharing helps to illustrate a point or paint a picture.

Why Career Happiness Map Coaching?

Why did I choose that name? Why focus on happiness, instead of success, power, money or fame?

Happiness is at the core of what we need as humans. It encapsulates what all those other qualities seek to bring into our lives.

Or at least we hope. So often we see examples of people who have oodles of success, power, money, and fame and they are not happy at all. Many of them are downright miserable.

Does that mean those things are bad and we shouldn't want them?

Hell no!!

It is my intention for everyone to have all those things, IF they are what you want and make you happy.

How will we know if we are seeking something that will destroy us, or lift us up to levels of joy we never thought possible?

Read on, and trust yourself to sort it out, one step at a time. It is my wish that you will walk away from this book with a deeper understanding of your personal happiness, and the understanding that work isn't external to life – it is one of the many threads that make up the tapestry of your whole existence.

Most of us need to earn money to provide for our basic needs, but our hunger for satisfying work, our life's purpose, is much deeper than survival.

So, let's jump into this fun, exciting, terrifying, and exhilarating journey into your true calling.

But first, a quick insight into why this work is so vital – via "the people's platform" – social media.

My Most Loved Facebook Post

When I quit my day job as a Technical Recruiter to focus on my career coaching and fiction writing businesses full time, I was beyond excited! So, like any modern woman with a smart phone and big news to share, I hopped all over social media to shout my announcement from the rooftops.

Here is what I posted on my personal Facebook page:

"Tomorrow is my LAST DAY at my day job.

Be prepared to hear about some BIG stuff happening in my author and career coaching worlds."

That's it. One of my shortest posts in all of posting history. I accompanied it with a cute graphic of a girl looking super excited.

This simple post received 208 likes and loves, as well as 122 comments CONGRATULATING me!

Now, I *did* say that I was quitting to pursue my career coaching and author businesses full time, which is surely exciting, but this post received more positive interaction than the ones I previously shared about my son graduating from college with honors, and my husband and I getting married!

What does that say about how people feel about their jobs and the world of work?

I think it says that a lot of people would like to quit their jobs and they wish they could figure out how to do it, too.

I'm sure many friends and family who replied were just happy for me (THANK YOU!!), but I know (because they privately messaged me) that many are envious of my choice and dissatisfied with their own careers.

Does the thought of quitting your job light you up like a 4th of July sky?

If the answer is YES, holy crap YES YES YES!!!!!!!!!! – then why aren't you doing it?

I know what you're saying – or at least some of the most popular reasons/excuses:

- I can't afford to quit.
- My family counts on me for health insurance.
- I paid X million dollars for my education to do this job.
- What will people say if I leave a perfectly good job?
- My partner/spouse/child/parent will be angry if I make a change.
- There are no good jobs out there.
- Everyone hates their job – it's normal.
- What if I do something new and I don't like it?
- I am not qualified to do anything else.
- I am too old to start over.
- I like my comfort zone.
- And of course, the biggest reason you are holding this book in your hands:
- I don't know what I want to do.

YIKES – what a list!

So, what's a Smart (but confused, scared, and a little bit lost) Chick to do!?

THE WORK.

Yes, you must do the work. But don't worry – we are going to do it together and it's going to be fun and exciting. Nothing worth having isn't a little scary or sometimes a LOT scary, but the growth on the other side of fear and doubt is truly magical.

In this book, I will show you how all these perceived obstacles, or even sometimes partially real challenges, can be not only overcome, but squashed like the disease carrying vermin they are!

The disease is the belief that you must stay stuck in the wrong career, and the cure is to turn that false and damaging lie on its head, and expose it for the big joy sucking, life wasting, passion stealing, potential limiting piece of poop it is!

Sorry for the graphic and/or borderline aggressive rant, but I feel so strongly that once you do this work, you won't even recognize the joyous, fulfilled, and peaceful woman you have become.

No – scratch that. You will not BECOME that woman. You will FIND her. She's already present inside of you, and we are going to join forces to draw her out of hiding to discover her dream work and love her life!

How to Use this Book to Discover YOUR Dream Work

I always laugh at this section of non-fiction books – I mean, it's a book, I'm going to read it. What the hell?

If you're anything like me, by now you are thinking, "Well, this is a nice story, but how will I freaking make this happen for real?"

Don't worry – this is not just a motivational 'rah rah' tome to get you all revved up with nowhere to go.

No way! Yes, you will be buzzing at a high vibration - BUT with a clear, carefully planned destination in mind.

My program is fun, actionable, and 100% realistic. I am not about fluff and sugar coating the truth with strategies and beliefs no mortal woman who lives in modern society could possibly implement and attain.

So, before we dig in, here is some advice (and things to remember) on how to get the most out of our time together on your journey:

- It is NOT impractical to begin with your inner self – it is vital!
- Grab a pretty journal and a kick ass pen – writing it down makes it happen!
- Leave your inner critic at the door – or preferably send her packing!
- Be open to new ideas – nothing changes if you don't change perspective!
- Your worries, fears, and doubts are not serving you, but they are normal!
- It's NEVER too late to love your career! And your life! It's all the same!
- Work Can and SHOULD be FUN!
- Don't give up before the big breakthrough – it's on its way!
- Every setback is temporary!
- A supportive, inspirational partner/tribe/circle of friends changes everything!
- We all need coaches and mentors to lift us up to the next level!
- Don't forget to laugh!

You have all the answers, knowledge and passion within you to discover, navigate, and elevate your career to a place where you aren't wishing away huge chunks of your life waiting for the weekend, vacation, or dare I say

– your retirement. EEK!!!!

I don't know about you, but I love to travel, and the road to my Career Happiness has been the most rewarding one I've ever cruised along.

There will be bumps and cloudy days along the way, but I promise you that the other side of this journey is smooth and sunny!

So, let's get your Tickets for this unique, once in a lifetime trip to your dream work!

How this Book is Organized

We are now about to get in the car, with you in the driver's seat, and hit the road.

You will need sustenance for the trip – so pack a water bottle, we might stop for wine and chocolate, and I will toss you a cupcake any time you're getting stressed out. For those of you who eat better than I do, we can munch on some carrots and a fruit smoothie – we'll need it for energy!

It is also vital to make the time for this work and to let others in your life know that you'll be gone here and there, as you go inward and explore the 6 Tickets to Career Happiness.

Don't worry, this book provides admission to all of them, and I will be your friendly and knowledgeable (and sometimes "tough love dispensing") guide!

The 6 Tickets to Career Happiness:

1. Courage
2. Clues
3. Clarity
4. Community
5. Compass
6. Confidence

Together these topics will provide an in-depth framework to allow you to FINALLY conquer your limiting doubts, uncover your exciting desires, erase your sticky confusion, form your supportive tribe, map your joyful path, and step into the beautiful, unique career that is meant for you and you alone!!

I know these are lofty goals, but get in and start the engine, sister. We are about to leave the excuses and limitations in the ditch!

Courage

What is Courage?

Courage: mental or moral strength to venture, persevere, and withstand danger, fear, or difficulty – Merriam Webster Dictionary

Hmm...I think there's a lot more to it, don't you?

Sure, there are certainly many real dangers and difficulties in the world and in our lives. I don't mean to downplay those or disrespect the courage shown by people who have overcome unbelievable wrongs – war, disease, abuse, abandonment, discrimination, etc.

And yes, there are some people who have even dealt with some of these things in the workplace. I get it, and you are among the Career Happiness Warriors I seek to help most passionately.

However, for the most part the fears that hold us back from discovering and living our ideal work life are not anywhere near as real as these atrocities.

In many cases, they aren't real at all. They are just the lies we have been told, or we have created, to hide behind and keep us stuck in the familiarity of our own little worlds.

There will always be fear associated with change – that's how we are wired as human beings. However, we can be afraid and brave at the same time.

So, what is holding you back from realizing your dreams? From figuring it out? From even starting?

The Number One Secret to Discovering Your Ideal Career is:

Overcoming Limiting Beliefs

Doesn't that sound simple and daunting at the same time?

I know, I've been there many times. I have been carrying around a truckload of limiting beliefs my whole life. But the good news is that when you shine a light on them you can quickly dismantle them and replace them with bright, shiny new beliefs that are true, good, and full of ass-kicking levels of motivation.

So, who are the voices in your head?

We like to think that as stable, well-adjusted women, we only have one voice in our heads, right? It's the stable voice of reason and good decision making, perfected by years of life experience and wisdom.

Ahem, let's get real.

No matter how smart, experienced, or well-adjusted we are, we all have the tendency to listen to the OTHER VOICES.

Let's examine those other voices - who they are, what they say, and why we might listen?

We don't exist in a vacuum, and all our relationships and societal influences create our narrative - the stories we are told, and then in turn we tell ourselves (and then we tell our children!)

This cycle of storytelling is an ancient custom in all cultures, and it can be a wonderful way to pass down wisdom, humor, love, and useful advice.

But when it comes from the negative places of fear, lack, judgment and ignorance - close your ears and RUN!

Unfortunately, much of this information is passed down to us when we are young and impressionable, and the Four Horsewomen of Bad Life Choices (fear, lack, judgment and ignorance) form much of our early beliefs about ourselves and what we can achieve in this world.

Now you may have had a very enlightened mother or grandmother, or some other person in your life who influenced you positively, and who did not entertain the

Four Horsewomen when they came to call.

Instead they spouted tales and advice from the Four Fairies of Infinite Possibility. They are abundance, courage, curiosity, and knowledge.

If that's the case you have a leg up on this work, but I am still willing to bet that once you left the womb of these smart, savvy ladies and ventured out into the big, bad real world you met some voices that fed you some garbage beliefs.

It's okay – it happens to all of us and the good news is that we can silence the lies and bathe in the truth!

Let's examine some limiting beliefs that you might hold when it comes to career change:

- It's too late to start over.
- I spent too much time and money on my degree to change careers.
- I face discrimination because of my sex/age/race/religion/sexual orientation.
- I am only qualified to do what I've been doing.
- No one will give me a chance to do something different.
- It will be too hard to adapt to a new career.
- No one will be able to match my salary.
- Companies want to replace experienced people with junior employees to pay less.
- I should be happy that I have a good job with benefits.
- Who am I to want more?
- It's greedy to try to earn more money.
- If I change jobs, I will have to work harder for less.
- I don't know where to begin.
- No one likes their job - we live for the weekends and vacations.
- Work can't be fun - that's why they call it work, not play.

I could go on forever.

Do any of these stories sound familiar? I have heard all of these from clients who feel trapped in the wrong career, and guess what?

None of them are true.

Now I know you might be thinking that I'm wrong, and that there is discrimination in hiring practices, and you really don't know where to start, and companies do make it hard for us to change careers.

Sure, some of these are *sometimes* true for *someone somewhere*, but just because there could be a grain of truth in an idea that doesn't mean we can't overcome it, or that it's valid for you.

Obstacles are just problems to be solved – there aren't any permanent ninety-foot concrete walls with snakes below and vultures above us!

If we want to have the career and life of our dreams, we must discount these negative voices and tell the Four Horsewomen to run off into the sunset and leave us alone with the Four Fairies. They are the keys to success and the life we want to live.

Let's try an exercise to dispel one of these common limiting beliefs.

It's too late to start over.

I hear this one A LOT!!

Let's apply the following questions to this belief and see how it holds up.

1. Where did this belief come from, and who told me this story?
2. Why do I believe it - where is the evidence?
3. How is this belief serving me?
4. If it's not, what positive belief can I tell myself to erase and replace it?

In the interest of "we are all in this together", here are my answers to these questions because like all of you, I have worried that it was too late.

Number 1: I learned at a young age that we should choose a career and do that one thing for the rest of our lives. My father and all the other adults in my life had one career path, and whether or not they liked it, they stuck with it until retirement. I thought that meant wanting change made someone a quitter, or a whiner, and that suffering was considered good for the soul. I saw this modeled and I also grew up at a time where most people in society were still following this career selection model. Trailblazers and out of the box thinkers were few and far between and I didn't know they existed.

And once I discovered them, I spent many years thinking they were liars, cons, and at best...dreamers - all things very much not respected in my circles. So, what did I do? I spent years beating myself up for bad decisions and miring in the shame of needing to "fix" my career, and therefore make myself an acceptable adult.

Number 2: I believed this information because people who I loved and trusted taught me to think this way - outwardly and by example. I had an ideal childhood in many ways - I always felt safe, loved, and cared for. So why wouldn't I take to heart everything that I learned from the adults in my life? I didn't even realize I was blindly believing these limiting ideas until I was MUCH older. And even now, in middle age, when I hear a new and out of the box idea I think - what would my ___ say about that? It's a much more fleeting detour to that thinking, but it still happens.

So where was the evidence that at some point it would be too late to start over? There wasn't any. I just didn't see any examples of people who had done it at all, let alone successfully! So, I assumed it was a monumental task that would be impossible to figure out, and if I didn't get it together by my thirties for sure, I was doomed.

Number 3: It 100% NEVER served me, but I was so busy believing it that it never occurred to me to seek to dispel this idea and prove otherwise. It was a done deal. And if anyone did model this behavior for me to see (in magazines, books, TV, on the new and confusing Internet), I just told myself that those people were lucky, or they had advantages I didn't have and couldn't obtain. And I should just stay where I was because that's where I chose to be and that's where I belonged now. Fun was for after hours, vacations and weekends - not the day to day of work.

Number 4: Luckily, my natural curiosity and stubborn tendency led me to rabbit holes of research and new ideas - books, movements, spiritual practices, teachers, and of course a growing knowledge and trust of how to find information on the Internet.

I invited the Four Fairies into my life and ravenously studied their new and exciting messages.

I began to break down all my limiting beliefs, about career and all other aspects of my life.

Now when I find myself butting up against a limiting belief (AKA obstacle) to getting what I want, I find that I only need to go through this exercise to dismantle the negativity and replace it with a positive belief.

You woke up today - therefore you can do anything you want.

There is no evidence that suggests that Career Happiness has an expiration date. You are alive and well and ready to pursue your dreams.

Your passion fuels your actions, not your age. The stories you were told *may* be words of wisdom, but they may just as easily be based in fear, lack, judgment, or ignorance.

It's okay that you once believed it- you probably had good reasons. But now you know better. Now you are a Career Happiness Seeker, and not only are you out of the box, there is NO box.

These beliefs are NOT serving you. If they were, you wouldn't be reading these words. Messages about finding your Career Happiness wouldn't resonate with you, unless it was just to smile and say – "I hope Carol can help all those people who are still stuck in the wrong career. But that's not me, I love my job."

So, since it *is* you (and that's OKAY!), we can fix it, and together we can get you on the road to your ideal working life. Where is your spot on the Career Happiness Map?

Read on sister, because we are about to find it – BUT first let's explore more ridiculous notions around fear and cultivate the courage to get to the juiciest parts of this process.

The Buzzy Bee

What are you afraid of?

When I was a little girl - probably about 3 (although I think I may have even been younger - that's how traumatic this was - I remember!), I received a Fisher-Price Buzzy Bee as a gift (I know I am dating myself!). It was a cute, age-appropriate toy, and I was TERRIFIED of it!!

I hid it at the bottom of my toy box and didn't tell anyone I didn't like it. It made a buzzy noise when you touched it a certain way, and I would accidently find it at the bottom of my toy box, make it buzz, and my terror would be reborn.

I recalled this fear when I was writing some content for my group career coaching program and I couldn't remember exactly what the Buzzy Bee looked like. Surely it must have been menacing since it was so incredibly scary to me. I do remember my little heart racing every time I saw it.

So, I Googled it and I couldn't believe my eyes. Surely, I was typing it in wrong. Or maybe I didn't have the name right – there was no way this toy could have been scary.

Take a moment and Google it, and look at this horrifying sight, if you dare!

Silly little girl, right? It's freaking adorable! Look at

the little smile! It has a crown, like a queen. She has flowers painted on her body. She's a beautiful, happy Queen BEE! If anything, this was an empowering symbol of girl power – way before its time!

So, why was I afraid?

Because I didn't know that it couldn't hurt me. I was always told to stay away from real bees as if they would kill me on contact.

Of course, telling children to avoid getting stung by a bee is good parenting, but I guess no one made the connection between those dangerous bees outside and this cute little toy bee, and how I might react.

I simply didn't have all the information I needed, and I was afraid to ask.

I also felt shame and guilt because if my parents gave me this toy it must be something I should like. I must have been weird or defective in some way if I didn't like this thing other kids liked.

I know - I was WAAAYYY too intense at 3!

The reason for sharing this is to show the parallels in my (and maybe your) adult life.

Have you ever been afraid to ask when you didn't understand?

Afraid to take a risk?

Ashamed or guilty about wanting more when society (or someone else) tells you that you should or shouldn't like or do something?

Do you ever feel bad about being different or wanting to make a different choice than the one you've already invested in?

Well, you need to embrace your Inner Buzzy Bee!

That cute little bug can remind you that you need to look beyond your fears, dig into them, gather information, uncover the truth, measure the real risk, and find joy!

Someday when I am a grandmother, I am going to buy my granddaughter a Buzzy Bee (if I can find one haha) and teach her to face her fears armed with data, confidence, and the curiosity to open herself up to life!

For now, I'd love to help you!

I am not going to give you a Buzzy Bee, but I will help you to overcome your fears, develop confidence, ask the right questions, and explore the answers.

And now that I'm thinking about it, I think I am going to try to find a Buzzy Bee on eBay for myself. It would be the perfect reminder that things are usually not as scary as we make them out to be, and I am more powerful than my limiting beliefs.

Grab that journal and start examining the confused little girl inside of you, and help her to see that she is smart, powerful, and wise.

Her Inner Buzzy Bee just needs some love and support from your grown-up, wise self.

The Four Horsewomen of Bad Life Choices – especially fear and ignorance want you to stay small – but let's just say no.

Two of the Four Fairies of Infinite Possibility – courage and knowledge – are about to take over and these ladies are truly magical.

What Buzzy Bees have you allowed to hold you back? And how can the Fairies help you take that first baby step out of your career ditch?

The "Uncomfort" Zone

Just how "comfortable" is it in your comfort zone?

Is it loaded to the brim with puppies/kittens, coffee/wine, cozy blankets, a warm fire, endless praise and fulfillment and a sense of accomplishment and the joy that comes from doing the work you love to do?

See what I did there?

I would be willing to bet that your comfort zone is actually quite uncomfortable.

If it wasn't, you wouldn't be reading about career development, complaining to anyone who will listen about your job, dreading Mondays, and fighting that knot in your stomach that is trying to tell you that you are meant for more.

You can do better…and you need to haul your butt out of your "Un-comfort Zone" and take some risks.

I'm not suggesting you take up a dangerous hobby that will almost certainly plunge you into injury, financial ruin, or an anxiety-ridden freak out!

One step at a time, woman!

No one is a bigger chicken than me – remember the Buzzy Bee?

Today I invite you to envision what your life would feel like if your comfort zone was truly comfortable, and you weren't lying to yourself to prevent your Inner Smart Chick from coming out to play and leading you into new and exciting places.

By now you have figured out that I assign names and visual symbols to concepts (imagine a cute baby chick wearing glasses).

Why? Because it makes the work more fun!

Getting out of your so-called Comfort Zone starts with play - not BIG SCARY HARD WORK!! Yes, career transformation will require work and dedication, but start with the FUN part. The exploration, the dreaming - but do it in a STRATEGIC way.

Yes, I know I always say work can be fun, and now I am saying that strategy can also be fun.

I'm turning fun on its head over here - but stay with me.

Once you begin to move beyond this notion of the Comfort Zone you will see it for the lying limiting belief that it is.

Sure, we are all a little afraid of change because it's the unknown.

But why does everything have to be known in order to be good? Haven't you had some amazing and wonderful surprises in your life?

Guess what? If you allow change and growth to enter your world in a big way, you will open the door for many more surprises – the kind that will move the needle forward on creating the career of your dreams.

So, unless you are currently bathing in a sea of comfort, give yourself the chance to explore

the alternatives. Grab your journal ladies, because we are about to dig a little deeper into finding the courage you need to launch your new work life.

What would make you feel a little uncomfortable right now – as it pertains to finding your ideal work?

Go do that thing. Write down a step you could take to move in that direction. Just one. I'll wait.

And when you're done, if you need a little more support, head over to my website (isn't it fun?), and send me a note to explore how I might be able to support you further:

http://careerhappinessmap.com/contact/

I'd love to hear what's been keeping you stuck and share how I can help you climb out of that career ditch.

I promise you that you can make that comfort zone look like a dirty shack in the woods with spiders and no running water, when you compare it to the life you can step into.

Career Role Models: Healthy, Toxic or Confusing

Who taught you about work? Who were your work role models? Did they work hard? Were they a bit lazy?

How about their attitude towards money? Did they work harder to make more? Did they prefer to save every dime, so they didn't have to work harder? Or make changes?

Was work more about service to others than making money? Was there greed involved?

Did your role models struggle to find work, keep work, or succeed at work? Or were they super successful and intimidating?

I was raised in a family of hard workers. My grandfather fixed cars in his driveway after he retired from working in construction in New York City. One of the "hands that built America" he was one of those children of immigrants with that amazing spirit of industry.

He grew up poor and worked his ass off for everything he had. The son of an alcoholic father and a tirelessly devoted mother of seven children, he never sat around waiting for something to happen. He was uneducated, but that didn't stop him from having a nice, modest home in the suburbs and all the things he needed in life.

His wife, my grandmother, never worked one day in her life for wages.

Yes, that's right – she left this earth never having earned a paycheck.

But she worked all the time. She cleaned her house every day, she planted flowers, cooked every meal, and even swept the street in front of her house. I am not kidding!

I spent a lot of time with this set of grandparents – my mother's parents. She learned the lesson of hard work well and kept our home spotless and was the hardest working wife and mother I knew growing up.

She quit her job when she was pregnant with me and that was the end of her career outside the home. But she never behaved like the stereotypical lazy housewife and she was an excellent role model for working hard and doing your best. She showed me the importance of devotion to your calling, and even though she did not inspire my career choices, she helped me to see the value of taking pride in your endeavors.

My father worked more than any human I have ever encountered. His career spans over five decades, and he is still working in his own consulting business after a long and successful career in banking. He constantly showed me an example of hard work and dedication, and a work ethic in business that is second to none. His confidence is contagious and taught me the power of applying myself to a vision.

I am a big ball of energy as a result of my genetic makeup. All these people and their industrious natures live within me.

So, why did I spend many years doing the wrong work and struggling in my career?

As you can imagine, I have given this question a lot of serious thought. I can't teach others how to find the root of their limiting beliefs without shining a bright light into my own dusty corners and faded memories.

I loved both of my parents equally, but I identified more with my father when it came to career, and our personalities were more similar. However, I was a girl and I identified strongly with my mother and her maternal side, which was her focus in life.

This created some confusion for me. I wanted to be like both of them, but how was I going to pull that off? Sure, there were lots of successful working women when I was finding my way in the eighties, but I also really liked having my mother at home, and I knew I wanted a family. There was never any doubt about that.

But how to put it all together was elusive, so I made decisions based on fear and insecurity, instead of opportunity and my own inner power.

Take some time to examine where your beliefs about work come from. Are they positive or negative? Helping or hurting? Do they serve you now? That's the most important question.

It's time to open your journal again and ask your Inner Smart Chick these revealing questions.

But don't spend a ton of time on this exercise. Don't DWELL on anything negative or yucky or uncomfortable that arises. Approach it from a place of curiosity, not judgment or shame (remember the Four Horsewomen we want to send off into the sunset?).

Once you have it figured out, just release what doesn't work, what doesn't really BELONG to you, and what may be holding you back.

Bless it and let it go.

Most of the time the people in our lives mean well. They tried. They were figuring out their own path and they had their own struggles. You may not even know about the root of their fears or pain or confusion.

But none of that is yours.

Free up that mental space to bring in the Four Fairies of Infinite Possibility - abundance, courage, curiosity, and knowledge.

I promise you'll feel lighter, and ready to design a career that is YOURS!

Working for the Weekend

If you spend your weeks saying things like…

- "Go away, Monday!"
- "Happy Hump Day – we're almost there!"
- "It's Friday, we made it."
- "I hate Sunday nights!"

then you are doing it wrong.

And by "it", I mean work. Life. All of it. Your whole existence.

I know that sounds harsh, but we need to face these uncomfortable realities to push past fear and doubt. The first part of solving a problem is to uncover its origins and blast it in the face with a new reality.

We live in a society where it's a source of humor to hate our jobs, and a badge of honor to "survive" to the weekend.

Are people really thinking they aren't going to make it to Friday? Is that in doubt? Unless you are a shark wrangler or a tightrope walker, you should feel certain that Friday is coming in its own time.

Do you really want to make fun of your unhappiness? Or congratulate yourself for only figuring out how to love less than half of your days on this earth?

And let's not forget how the "Monday Blues" come

creeping in on Sunday! Many people really can only relax from Friday night to Sunday morning.

So essentially you own 1.5 days of your life each week.

Um...that is not acceptable to me. And I know you feel the same way. You just haven't dug yourself out of the hole yet. You haven't accepted that there is another way, and it's on the other side of fear – the vast majority of which is buried under tons of outdated, untrue limiting beliefs.

So, what do you do? You post "Hump Day" memes on Wednesday of Snoopy cheering, and "We Made it to the Weekend" graphics of a fist pumping baby.

And of course, TGIF has been a common expression as long as I can remember. A whole restaurant chain named themselves after this desperation to make it to the weekend. I often wonder if they did any business during the week. After all, they were telling us that fun and burgers and beer can only be properly enjoyed after the evil work week has come to its miserable end.

Even Loverboy gave us "Workin' for the Weekend" in the 80's. But even though I loved those long-haired, eyeliner wearing hotties, they were wrong.

Yes, I said it. Loverboy was wrong. And so are all the disillusioned people who have collectively decided to hide behind jokes and a shared "misery loves company" mentality to mask their pain and make excuses for not pursuing their gifts and passions.

Well, not today Loverboy! Or tomorrow. Or any day that I or any Smart Chicks who are reading this book have a say. We will not succumb to this ridiculous notion that if we are all unhappy together, it's okay.

Let's kill the "cat dangling from a tree" Monday memes, and get you on your path to living every day fully. That is where I am today, and if my husband wasn't home on the weekends, I seriously would not know one day from the next. They all rock harder than an 80's hair band!

When it seems like there is no way out, sit down and make a list, in your pretty journal, of all the challenges in your life that you never thought you'd overcome, all the things you thought you couldn't do, and all the things you have today that you only dreamed of in the past.

Here is a sample of my list to get you started:

- Got out of retail management into a talent acquisition career with no experience.
- Became a dog mom at 41, despite being very allergic for my whole life.
- Remarried after ten years of single motherhood and horrendous dates.
- Kept my house and my sanity on my own after my divorce.
- Completed my master's degree as a working single mom.
- Moved into a more fulfilling role at work by asking for it.
- Launched my son into a successful career/ life pursuing his passion.
- Published 8 novels to date, after a lifetime of fear of rejection.
- Quit my day job and started my career coaching business.
- Became a dog mom to another adorable wiener dog.
- Sang in public.

And I know I'm not done.

I will let you in on a little secret – everything I do that is worth doing scares me. Sometimes a little, sometimes a lot.

But I have learned that the secret to moving the needle on your fears is shifting your focus away from them, getting to the root, and reframing them by looking for clues that they are the big pile of crap that they most surely are.

I'm sure you might be thinking that some fear keeps

you safe. But that's not fear. That's caution, sense, planning, reasonable goals. Those are all good things. Do you know how to tell the difference?

You can move forward with all those things for company, and still make strides towards your goals.

But not fear. When you are deep in fear, it is crippling. Paralyzing. Immobilizing.

And sure, it's possible to feel some fear and forge on. As I said I do it every day. But I'm moving forward. Sometimes in baby steps and other times in bigger leaps. That's all part of the execution of the plan, which we will get into in a later section.

Therefore, I am not giving in to fear.

Right now, I want you to work on dismantling the fearful voices and replace them with their more positive counterparts.

Remember the Four Fairies? Invite them in. In case you have forgotten their names, they are abundance, courage, curiosity, and knowledge.

Focusing on abundance (all the things you have and have achieved and overcome) builds courage. It takes the light off fear and leaves it in the dark corner where it belongs.

Curiosity and knowledge will come out to play in time, but courage is the real gate buster.

If you want to love all your days, you need to disavow yourself of this concept that hating the workweek is a socially binding, fun way to look at life.

It's not. It just keeps you down there with the people who are just "making" it.

And you want to do far more than that or we wouldn't be getting to know each other.

So, what do you need to do?

Decide to start.

"That's it? Just do it? You're giving me a sportswear slogan, Carol?"

Yes, I am. It's good advice. And I'll tell you why.

Decide to Start

I decided to call my career coaching business Career Happiness Map because moving from where you are to where you want to be in your career does not usually happen in one step.

It *can*, and you may be one of the people who is farther along on the map and *now* you're ready for the final step. But if you look back at the path behind you, it's usually long, and had a lot of detours, wrong turns, and even some forays into ditches on the side of the road.

And that's okay because hopefully you've learned something from all the steps and missteps along the way. Every so-called failure is an opportunity to learn and perfect your process.

So, decide to start - s*omething*.

Take the class, read the book, ask for the informational interview. Talk to your boss about more or different responsibilities, apply for the business loan. Sketch your designs, hire a website designer, research moving to that city you're always thinking about.

Do SOMETHING!

So often I hear people saying that they aren't taking an action because that action alone won't get them where they want to be. It won't be enough, so why bother?

Well, of course not. How often does ONE action get you anywhere doing anything?

That's like saying you can't cook spaghetti because putting the water in the pot isn't going to make it happen.

Or you can't drive to work because the turn out of your driveway won't get you there.

Or you can't find a life partner after one date, so you don't want to meet any new people.

Nothing is completed in one step. You can't even go to the bathroom in one step.

You need a map. A plan. Planning is not a bad word. There is nothing more fun than planning for your exciting future, unless you invite the Four Horsewomen of Bad

Decisions to the planning party.

Do yourself a favor and don't let fear, lack, judgment, and ignorance crash your party and mess up your progress. All they do is drink too much, eat all the food, and try to get you to abandon your hopes and dreams for their sucky version of reality.

Send those bitches down to the nearest dive bar and surround yourself with the Four Fairies – those ladies know how to throw a glam party and keep it going.

Remember, you're not leaping off a cliff. No one is telling you to quit your job tomorrow and live in a trash can working on your big idea. You can take baby steps at first, and as you move through the 6 Tickets to Career Happiness Discovery (http://careerhappinessmap.com/work-with-carol/#discovery), you will gain momentum.

When you first learn how to do anything, you do it slower than others who have been at it for years. That's normal.

You know how when you go to a Pilates class and everyone is strong and in shape and you feel like your limbs are going to snap off and your lungs are caving in?

Hmm, that might just be me after a period of exercise-free time. But you get the picture. After I go to class consistently for a while, I am stronger, and I feel so much better.

The same is true when I am making videos of myself and posting them on social media, doing public speaking, and publishing new books and asking people to review them.

At first, it's horrifying and then it becomes easier, and then it's fun and rewarding.

Fear becomes a distant memory. And courage grows and drives me forward.

So just start. I'll be here with you. Helping you figure this out is my life's work so there is plenty more support and guidance where this came from.

Now that we are dismantling the false beliefs, and claiming our power, what do we do next?

Part of the fear of deciding to start is that we don't know where to begin. We don't know where we're going.

We can't cook the spaghetti because we aren't sure that's what we want for dinner. The car isn't going to drive itself to its destination, so we must plug the address in the GPS. And how can we start dating if we don't know what we want in a partner, or where to find good prospects?

On to the next Ticket to Career Happiness Discovery (http://careerhappinessmap.com/work-with-carol/#discovery). The juiciest of them all:

Clues.

I told you we wouldn't wallow in the fear/courage section for long.

You've got dreams to manifest, so let's dive in.

Clues

Clues – Where the Hell are They?

Clue: a piece of evidence or information used in the detection of a crime or solving a mystery – Merriam Webster Dictionary

At first, I hesitated to share this definition because crimes and mysteries are not what careers are all about.

Then I thought about it a little more. It surely feels like a crime to spend your life doing work you dislike, and it is often a mystery as to what you want to do.

And then of course the actual *doing* of the thing is even more elusive.

But we'll get to that in later chapters.

Right now, we are going to focus on uncovering the Clues to your ideal work.

Most of us who are unhappy with our jobs spend a lot of time thinking about this problem, but just thinking doesn't get us very far. It tends to produce more anxiety and some sleepless nights. And for some - binge eating and TV watching.

Our thoughts race around aimlessly, or they whip around in a circle. If you're anything like me, my mind can take me on a roller-coaster to hell in a flash, and all my problem-solving skills go out the window as I devolve into worry and a feeling of hopelessness.

Somewhere along the way I learned to write things down.

Well, I actually *wrote* all the time as a child. That was my long-buried dream, and I am happy to report that at age 45 I finally wrote a book. I have now written 8 novels and 2 short story collections, and this book, with no plan to stop.

Ever.

Even though this was my biggest childhood activity, once puberty hit I stopped writing – creatively or in any kind of journaling capacity. My anxiety took over and all I did was think and overthink about my problems, limitations, and fears.

It took me many years to crawl out of that hole and begin to do the necessary work on myself to dig into my deepest desires and create the career/life of my dreams.

It's *always* a work in progress, but I have moved ahead by leaps and bounds on all the many things I worried about as a young adult and a grown woman.

The kind of writing that will help you on this path (It completely transformed my life!) is journaling.

Now I know some of you don't like to write, or you find writing to be hard, or boring.

Maybe it's been years since you've written more than a random thought down on a piece of paper, and everything longer than that is communicated into your phone's voice activation.

But there is a great shift that takes place in the mind when you write with a pen and paper. That's why I have been prompting you so far in this book with small directives to answer some questions in writing.

But now in the Clues phase, we are going to write a lot more.

This type of writing does not have to be perfect. It's better if it's not. Don't worry about spelling, punctuation or grammar, unless you want to.

This is for your eyes only. When I work with 1:1 Career Happiness Discovery (http://careerhappinessmap.com/work-with-carol/#discovery) clients, I give them worksheets to complete and return to me. Those thoughts help me to frame better questions for the client and guide them to quicker and more effective solutions.

However, there are other times when I ask them to

write about something without sending it to me. That uncensored writing is for the client only. This is where the deepest "ah ha" moments come to life.

Sometimes I write about the same issues for a couple of pages before a lightbulb flashes in my head and I get an idea that begs to be explored.

You need a little patience. You also need quiet and privacy, both to be alone with your thoughts without interruption, and so you don't worry about someone looking over your shoulder or asking what you're writing.

In this section I am going to help you to unearth the Clues, some of them from a long time ago, that form your deepest vocational desires.

I call this the dreamy phase because we are not running any of this through the lens of reality yet. So, please do not analyze anything that comes up and say things like:

- "Well I loved doing that when I was a kid, but that won't make me any money."
- "I used to do that, but I'm not good at it anymore."
- "There is no market for that skill."
- "I don't have time to develop in that area."
- "No one will ever hire me to do that now."

It is not time for all of that. We will get to the point in the process where we are designing your Career Happiness Map, and then we will be forced to become more practical around where you want to go and how you are going to get there.

The problem with applying this serious, logical approach to Career Happiness Discovery at the beginning of the process is that it cuts creativity off at the knees before it has any chance to run and see where it might take you.

Perhaps your initial idea is over the top or unrealistic, but there may still be Clues in the clue (I told you we are going deep!) that can lead you to a career you had not thought of before.

Most of us are very limited in our knowledge of what is possible in the world of work, especially those of us who have spent many years in one field and haven't given any real consideration to what's going on in the career space.

So, please grab your journal and a pen that writes smoothly and effortlessly, and let's get to writing things down and making them happen for you.

But first I want to tell you a quick story about how I was first introduced to the world of work, and what that taught me about the value of loving your job.

Or not.

Silly Girl in the City

When I was in high school, growing up in the Hudson Valley area in New York, my father worked for a large bank in New York City.

He ended up working there for his entire career, and his tales of working life were the main ones I had feasted on as a child.

I say "feasted" because I romanticized the city and working in a big building. It seemed so glamorous and exciting and I longed to be a part of that world. My father worked very hard, as I had previously mentioned, and I wasn't sure how I was going to feel about that part, but I wanted to be immersed in that culture - and go to lunch at cool New York delis and work late and order Chinese food, and get bagels and...

Okay, a lot of my fantasies involved food, but they also involved wearing smart suits and pumps and making big decisions and making a lot of money.

Unfortunately, I never ran ANY of that through the lens of reality, even when I had the chance to see it up close and personal.

My first job at 16 was a summer Internship at my father's company, at an office he used to work at, reporting to his former boss.

666 Fifth Avenue. That was my building. I was in New York recently and there is now a fast food place and a chain clothing store on the ground floor of this historic building, and who knows what is on the many upstairs floors.

But I know it no longer houses the company I worked for.

This was a prime location – near Central Park and St. Patrick's Cathedral. I felt insanely lucky to have this opportunity since my friends were all working at fast food restaurants in our little dinky hometown.

Every morning my father and I got up at five, and I primped my enormous hair with a third of a can of hairspray (it was 1984) and we got in the car for our 1.5-hour commute.

Many people who lived in our area worked in the city and while that drive might seem insane to many, it was very normal for my family and many others who earned good salaries and had serious careers, but wanted to live far enough away to afford a nice house.

I would get to my father's office with him at about 7:30. Most mornings we would stop and get some breakfast in the company cafeteria and a little before 9 I would walk from his office on Lexington Avenue to my office on 5th.

Even that solo walk felt indulgent. I was moving with the energy of the city and I watched all the women in their suits and sneakers, with their huge briefcases and bags containing their chic office footwear.

I worked answering the phones for a sales department. I believe they were selling investments to individuals. Some clients were small potatoes, but many were wealthy and had a lot of money at stake.

Many were also demanding and rude and crazy. But, so were the salespeople.

One of the first things I noticed was that many people were nowhere near as excited as I was to be there. They were angry and smashed the pushpin hard into the bulletin board where I had secured their handwritten phone messages.

I would tell my father about the things that went on in the office (after all he used to work there and many of these people had previously reported to him), and more often than not he would say that they were lazy, unfocused, and not very good at their jobs. That's why they were disgruntled employees.

Now that I look back, I can see there were many other reasons for their dissatisfaction, some of which were valid. I am also certain that most, if not all, of those people chose that work because they thought it would make them a lot of money, their parents pushed them into it, or some other reason that had zero to do with their passions.

I should have looked at this situation as a learning experience. Instead of letting myself get sucked into something I would hate, I had the opportunity to do whatever I wanted. I had begun looking at colleges and I had lots of interests.

But none of them had anything to do with that type of career.

I didn't want to be a business major. I hated math and the thought of accounting made me ill. I had no technical interest or ability, so the blossoming information technology side of business was not calling my name either (although there was a hot guy who worked at my summer job in front of a computer and what he did was super mysterious. But hot).

Sales seemed scary and although I was outgoing, I couldn't see myself doing that type of work. But still I held on to this idea that whatever I did needed to be surrounded by money and prestige, or else I would be wasting my intelligence and skills.

That fall when we began looking at colleges, I was thinking of majoring in psychology. I was also interested in journalism.

While my parents were not opposed to those majors, the world seemed to be telling me that I would not make money in those fields. Unless I went on to get a Ph.D. in psychology, I wouldn't be able to do much with that degree in the money department, and I did not want to commit to that many years of school. My baby making clock was already ticking when I was a little girl, absorbing my mother's maternal side.

And in the 80's, journalists were guys who sat typing in a smoky room reporting on crimes or politics, of which I had no interest, and the magazines were full of super chic and polished city chicks who were well connected - and still apparently didn't make a lot of money.

Or so I thought.

So, I was stuck with no good plan. I knew I didn't fit in with the people I watched work in banking, but I still longed to be a part of something lucrative. I had given up on the idea of being a lawyer by the time I was twelve, and doctor was out as my science grades were abysmal and I couldn't even look at a little cut without getting sick.

I'm not going to tell the rest of this tale in detail, like how I really screwed up by pursuing none of these choices for a very long time in favor of a relationship that was to produce an amazing child, but ultimately lead me down paths that were not right for me.

I don't blame that relationship, or that man, however. We are all in charge of our own choices. I made bad choices out of confusion, fear, and insecurity.

So, let's dig into your reasons and flip them on their heads. Still have your journal handy?

Good, we are about to poke around in the past and in your present subconscious – but as much as that sounds like it could suck, I promise you it can be very fun if you check all of your misgivings, worries, and cynicism at the door. Just give them to me, I'll hold them. And when we are done, I know you won't want them back.

Your Inner Smart Chick

Feeling stuck is hell. I've been there many times.

But it's an illusion. You are very rarely actually *stuck* in any situation. It's a choice - one that is usually fueled by fear, lack of information, and sometimes your own stubborn will to make something work just because at one time you chose it.

But who gives a crap?

You have the freedom to choose and choose again. Make choices until you get to where you want to be. Don't stay stuck in in the mindset of lack and scarcity and "It's too hard" and "I don't know what to do" and "It's too late."

These are all excuses that just keep you where you are. They are not real limitations.

And you know what? Once you tell those voices to shut up, you will soar. Once you free yourself from that stuck feeling, you will freaking bounce off the walls and fly towards your dreams.

Or at least in their general direction.

Everything will seem easier. Once you start. So where should you start?

With dreaming.

I know you are thinking this is supposed to be an actionable career guide so why the hell are we indulging in "la la land" activities?

Be patient. Remember I said we start with dreaming. We aren't going to lounge here for all time and stare out the window while life passes us by.

Chances are you've already done some of that (I know I have!) and dreaming is only helpful to achieve our goals when you take the information cultivated in this stage and move it through the next stages – which I PROMISE we will get to.

Now that we've worked through some limiting beliefs, armed you with more courage to move forward, and defined the Clue discovery process, let's dive in.

So, again. Why dreaming?

Dreaming is fun (and remember how work CAN and SHOULD be fun?).

It's especially enjoyable to daydream about all the nice things we'd like to have, places we want to go, and things we want to see and do and experience.

You know what else is fun?

Actually, LIVING our dreams. And in real life, that requires a plan. A MAP.

Planning gets a bad rap, especially from people who see it as something that curbs their spontaneity and takes up all their time.

But a good, well-crafted plan frees you to live your life the way you want to. It creates more time for the things and people you love.

Nothing wastes time and energy like going after a dream all willy nilly. Willy nilly is not fun because it ends up creating anxiety and failure.

And not the good kind of failure where you learn from your mistakes and continuously improve. I'm talking about the bad kind where you give up. And we are not giving up! RIGHT?

Imagine what would happen if you let your Inner Smart Chick guide your career choices?

Remember her?

Yes, I know that's a silly name, but it's more fun than Wise Self or Inner Sage.

We all have a woman inside of us who knows WAY more than we do on the surface, if we would just let her out to play. She knows what she wants, but you're not listening to her. So, let's turn off our Inner Mean Girl (she sucks) and let our Inner Smart Chick run wild!

One of the reasons I don't believe in using traditional career assessments/tests in my coaching practice is because they TELL you what you should do instead of asking YOU the right questions so that you can tell YOURSELF!

I know you still might be thinking that you don't know the answers, but somewhere inside, you do. I promise.

And at the very least, you know what makes you feel inspired, happy, fulfilled - what you love doing. And if you still don't think so, then we are going to have to dig even deeper to rescue your unique, wise, and talented Inner Smart Chick.

I ignored mine for years, and now that I've unleashed her my workdays are full of fun and creativity, and I feel energetic and fully ME!

So, let's go back a bit in your life and rewrite your Career Happiness story.

Journals UP!

WHO Do You Want to BE When You Grow Up?

When you were a child, how did you answer that favorite question of every adult you met?

"What do you want to be when you grow up?"

Hmm...brings back some memories, right? I think most adults ask this question when they see a child because they don't know what else to ask them, other than the other favored gem of kids everywhere – "How's school?"

I think this question is flawed. Or at least it is limiting and misleading. If we are asking kids what they want to *be*, we should be asking them what they actually want to BE - what they want their lives to look like. And THEN start to help them explore what possible career fields might serve their vision of their ideal, happy lives.

Of course, this changes as kids grow, and it's a good process to revisit. Most adults don't know how to assist the children in their lives with these big questions, and the school counselors are often overworked and tied to a system that doesn't allow for the type of growth and self-reflection over time necessary to make good life choices.

When you were asked that question by most adults in your life, the person asking probably meant "what career do you want to pursue?"

When posing this question to someone in later high

school, or even college, this question is a tough ask. To ask a small child is just silly. Although, I remember people asking me before I started school!

When you're five years old you have only heard of like five jobs - whatever your parents do, and policeman, fireman, teacher, doctor, and ballerina/astronaut (dreams were very gender specific in my youth).

While these are all worthy pursuits, if we don't help kids dig deeper, it's a fruitless discussion. Is it no wonder as adults we often find ourselves confused, and still asking this question?

As you ponder how you responded to this question as a child, look for Clues as to what your answer *really* said about what you *value*, what *excites* you, and what has meaning for you.

But also think about the most vital question - what do you want to BE? Not do, work as, or pursue? First, start with what and who you want to BE in the world. This is the foundation.

I want to be someone who uses my gifts to create happiness and value for myself and others.

That's my mission statement of sorts. My vision. My guiding principle.

Call it whatever you want but starting with who you want to be and what you want to contribute to the world, in your unique way, is a valuable jumping off point as we dig for Clues into your ideal work. It gives you a baseline upon which to measure all your ideas and possible paths.

See, I told you all this "woo woo" stuff gets practical fast.

Now with your Inner Smart Chick as the one holding the pen to paper, let's introduce her to someone who can help her make leaps and bounds in the initial Career Happiness Discovery process.

Your 10-Year-Old Self

When you think about what you want to do with your career, sometimes it's hard to think about what you actually WANT to do. Or LIKE to do. Or dare I say - LOVE to do!

As we age, we tend to lose touch with what excites us in favor of what pays the bills, takes care of our family, conforms to societal and family expectations, etc.

But you know who totally knows what you LOVE?

Your ten-year-old self.

That little chick is *multi-passionate,* and she gets up every day ready to rock all her dreams and interests and she kills it!

When I was that little girl, I knew what I wanted, what mattered, and what lit me up.

Of course I didn't have the answers about how to put it all together as an adult, and I surely lost touch with her once puberty reared its ugly head, but despite wearing glasses, being teased for being too skinny, and frequently humiliating myself in gym class with my inability to do a cartwheel, I was confident and I pursued my passions.

Every day!

When I did this exercise recently, I was able to connect all the dots between what I loved to do and how I had FINALLY manifested a career life I love!

I had never thought to visit with her until I started my career coaching practice, and up until then I had truly figured everything out the hard way, through painful and confusing trial and error.

When I was a child I LOVED to write, and I gave it up when I went to junior high, and I published my first book at 46. That was kind of an easy dot to connect, so I felt like that was the big puzzle piece, and I had it all figured out and my exercise into delving into the deep past was done.

Then I remembered. And a whole additional layer

came to light.

I loved to play school with my little sister, who was 6 when I was 10.

I would make lesson plans for her and stand up in the front of the room and teach her.

I would do research on my lessons and make quizzes.

I even had a couple of friends who were willing to play this game with us. I am certain that my friend Maria is now a rocket scientist or a brain surgeon due to her intelligence and willingness to play school at a Saturday night sleepover.

But despite recalling this childhood fun, I know for sure that I never wanted to be a teacher. Of children. In the public-school system.

BUT - I love training, speaking, engaging audiences, and motivating people to learn and grow.

I just prefer to do it with adults.

I was amazed by the power of this exercise, and I wish I had tapped into my little girl wisdom a LONG time ago because the Clues were right there all along.

My hope for you is that you save yourself time and energy by having a talk with "little you".

As you can see, peeling back the layers uncovers vital Clues and digging deeper into those "ah ha" moments produces juicy nuggets of useful information.

Don't just think about what you were *doing* – clearly, I didn't want to be a teacher, and I thought writer was out as a serious occupation due to instability.

But upon further inspection, the activities and skills used to play school gave me much insight into what I enjoy and value.

Here's another example.

My friend Lauren and I loved to play superheroes in my backyard. This is prior to my ten-year-old self as we moved from that neighborhood when I was 9.

My sister was all about joining in on this one, and when she was as little as 3, she liked to pretend to be the "Beeonic Woman."

Lauren and I usually wanted to be Wonder Woman, Batgirl, or a character we created – Queenie. Unfortunately, we don't remember much about Queenie and her specific powers, but a few years ago we discussed this time period on Facebook, and Lauren remembered the name.

Why is this relevant? "Superhero" is obviously not a viable career choice, unless you want to play one in a movie, and if so that's a pretty cool goal.

It's relevant to us because of the skills and experiences we were emulating running around my backyard, pretending to have powers and capes and bullet deflecting bracelets.

Superheroes are powerful women. Leaders. They get shit done. They are fearless.

And those are the qualities I have reclaimed as I started my business, leaving the (false) security of the corporate world and a predictable paycheck behind.

I could share many more examples, but I think you see the value of having this deep chat.

Once you do, please record it in your journal and begin to connect the dots. You can make lists, diagrams, charts, or draw pictures.

Whatever way you process the info on paper is up to you. It's for your eyes only. So be very honest with yourself.

The little girl inside of you will appreciate you giving her a voice.

Once you have unearthed some of these Clues, let's move on to another important facet of Career Happiness Discovery in the form of a simple question.

Asking yourself this important question will deepen the experience further and help you to see the meaning in your dreams and desires. And it's a foundational piece to return to when things get hard, because as you know – they always do. This work is equipping you with tools to break through and connect with what matters.

What is your WHY?

Why?

It's a good question. Little kids ask it constantly. I remember when my son reached the age when all he did was ask why. And every single answer just created another why.

"Nick, come on honey, we have to go in the car now."
"Why?"
"We have to go to the grocery store?"
"Why?"
"Because we need food."
"Why?"
"We need food to live."
"Why?"

And this is how a simple shopping trip turns into a biology lesson. And anyone who knows me knows that science is not my thing.

Thank goodness he didn't need me to answer all his questions or else he'd be misinformed about a lot of things. When he was two or three his father told him not to ask Mommy the names of animals because she only know pig, cow, and horse.

Sadly, this was partially true.

Little kids ask why because they want to learn. They are little sponges soaking up information.

If you were a little sponge, what could you soak up? What would you want to know? Do? Be? Have?

You know I'm going to say it.

Why?

For instance, when I was loving running around my backyard playing superheroes with Lauren and my sister, why was that so awesome?

I enjoyed the feeling (here we go with the deeper stuff!) of being powerful, feeling free and in control. I craved the comradery of the other "superheroes" and working as a team.

When I was a pretend teacher, I liked being the center

of attention. I enjoyed feeling respected and smart.

Writing allowed me to use all the thoughts in my head to create something that never before existed. I felt creative and full of life when I told a story no one had heard. I liked to entertain and make people laugh.

It's the *feelings* that tap into the "why".

Sometimes getting in touch with your "why" when it comes to your career is as simple as asking the right questions.

- Why are you unsatisfied in your work?
- Why do you need that?
- Why is it important to do work that you love?
- Why has it been difficult to discover your calling? To put a plan into action?

Carve out some introspective time this week and do the "why" exercise as if you were a cute, inquisitive four-year-old playing on your mom's last nerve. You are bound to be surprised and inspired.

Now let's start applying some of these Clues to the present.

I told you we wouldn't hang out in the past for long – we have a Career Happiness Map to create!

Less or More

You're probably used to seeing that phrase as "More or Less", right? It looks weird the other way around.

Stay with me and I'll explain why I think it makes more sense this way when you're assessing what you want in your career. It's a productive exercise to sit down with your journal and make a list of what you want *less* (or NONE) of in your career, and what you want *more* of in your work.

So why are we tackling *less* first? It's kind of a downer to start with the yucky stuff first. But what we attack we conquer, ladies!

If you focus on what you want *less* of first, you are eliminating the crap and cleaning the slate to bring in what you want *more* of. And what you want more of is what you want to *concentrate* on. Your time and attention should be focused on the good. The "more".

And the things you don't want – the "less" - are erased with all the good thoughts and plans that come from applying your newfound Clues to your daily life.

If you end the exercise with what you want less of, you're filling your mind with feelings of lack and negativity.

If you close your journal with the feelings of hope and possibility, and maybe even the beginnings of a GOAL or a PLAN or a MAP (like a Career Happiness Map), then you'll feel amazing, energized, motivated, and ready to get what you want!

Ending with the juicy stuff makes you hungry for more and basking in the glow of abundance.

So, what do you want less of, and what do you want more of? Let those feelings of "more" wash over you. More abundance, freedom, creativity, time, money, travel, etc.

Don't yet think about whether it's realistic. We are not there yet. For all of you logical, practical types, I promise it's coming.

Just indulge me a little longer and I promise that you are laying the foundation upon which to build an impenetrable fortress of rock-solid plans that are grounded in reality.

But first deeply examine your workdays and allow yourself to feel how all the tasks, responsibilities, activities, and interactions affect you.

What makes your stomach hurt?

What washes over you with a sense of accomplishment?

When I was sitting at my desk at my last job, I did a lot of work with this exercise. I had a good position doing work I knew how to do, working with and for good people, and I had more freedom and flexibility than most corporate employees since I worked from home.

So, what was wrong?

I wanted less structure and more freedom. I wanted *total* freedom.

Wonder Woman doesn't live by clocks and rules.

I wanted to lead, but not by managing people. I wanted to lead people to live better lives.

I wanted more creativity. Creativity all the time. I wanted to design new worlds, new people, and tell their stories.

I wanted to put my message before people to promote engagement and foster change.

My truth.

I knew the only way I could achieve the results of my Less or More exercise was to start my own business.

For you, it will be something entirely different.

Even if you also conclude that the entrepreneurial life is for you, it will be designed in a unique way that is an expression of your talents, desires, and experiences.

If it's a different job, work environment, or career field altogether, that will also be uniquely you.

The purpose of this work is to guide you to create the work you love, instead of looking to the external source of corporations and other organizations to offer you their premade, packaged version of what you should want in a career.

The only thing to remember is that work CAN and SHOULD be *fun*. And with some inner work, dedication, and guidance, you can get there, no matter what wrong turns or bad decisions you've made.

Who cares about all of that now? You can't worry about the past if you want to move forward to the career of your dreams.

So, let's get you on the right path. And start sketching out that Career Happiness Map.

Now that you know what you want more of, you can dare to dream of manifesting it into reality. You are ready to put more parameters around what that ideal working life looks like on a day to day basis.

Get ready to be a star!

Star of Your Own Life

Have you ever dreamed of being in a movie? On the stage?

That was another thing I had a wish for when I was very young - before teen awkwardness hit me hard, and I retreated. I have a whole story about playing the Mother Rabbit in the Peter Rabbit play in 3rd grade, but that's a tale that works better to illustrate an important point in another section.

For now, let's just talk about you. Whether or not you've ever wished to be in the limelight, you've surely had daydreams about what your life could be.

Right? Or do you not allow yourself to dream? To get your hopes up?

Today I invite you to suspend all reality (it's no fun otherwise) and think about the movie of your life - with you starring as the leading lady. Let those hopes soar into the heavens!

Only YOU get to write the script from here on out. Is it a rom com? A drama? An adventure? A mystery?

Who are the supporting characters? Where do you live? What do you do for fun? How do you serve others? How do you indulge yourself in joy and comfort? What are you doing to achieve this amazing life? What is the work you were born to do?

If it feels like a fantasy you are surely in your dream career.

Now, I know it's easy to fall into the trap of fantasizing so much that the exercise seems to be fruitless. You know what you're wishing for is slightly over the top. But that's okay. There are still *Clues* in that fantasy life. In that movie script.

Look for the deeper meanings of what you long for,

and always return to the "why".

If you want to work on the beach, WHY?

Maybe you enjoy warm weather, being outdoors, the sensory experience of the beach, being near water, the people you imagine will be there with you, etc.

Once you dig deeper you may find there are ways to get some of the things you want - right where you are. Or maybe you need to move, go back to school, explore a new field, or start your own business.

Our ideal lives can require big change.

We will discuss a bunch of those possible life changes to help you move the needle on your dream work in the section on Confidence. That's also where you will hear about my first (and last) starring role in a musical production. I know you can't wait now.

I know change can be scary. If you're feeling a little anxious about where this process is leading, refer back to the section on Courage. It's okay to feel apprehensive – this inner work can be exciting and make you want to throw up at the same time.

If that's how you feel as you uncover your Clues, you're doing it right.

And you'll be fine. I know you're up for it all because you are reading this book. You are reaching out for a framework to guide you to Career Happiness.

And I'm here for you – remember this is *my* life's work.

So, don't you want to be the star of your own life?

I thought so.

Now that you have a better idea of what your ideal workday and career look like, let's see what help you still need.

Career Genie in a Bottle

If you found a Genie in a bottle, what three wishes would you make to move your career plans forward? To create the life you dreamed of in the previous section? (If you didn't get anywhere with that exercise, I highly suspect it's because you just read the words and didn't pause with your journal to do the work! Go back and do it, I'll wait.)

If you did come up with an exciting career movie, what changes would you make in order to get there? What help do you need? Where are the gaps and how could you fill them?

Give yourself some time to explore your deepest desires. This is a fun exercise - don't overthink it or apply judgment or fear to the answers, BUT I would encourage you to try to reach beyond the unimaginative answers you would see in a movie or book about a Genie:

- I want to work on the beach.
- I want to earn a million dollars.
- I want to be a Queen.

These are good goals for someone, but maybe not you. I invite you to be a bit more creative and *personal* about the whole exercise. You can still reach for the stars without being a cliché.

Instead try to focus on your *deeper* wants - what would provide the most joy and meaning?

What would make you want to jump out of bed to get started?

Make you lose track of time?

What would make you feel proud, fulfilled and living in service to your highest good and use of your gifts?

Again, don't worry if it's realistic right now. Just think what you need to move forward. What small steps can you take to realize one of those wishes, since the Genie is just a metaphor?

You are your own Genie in this exercise. And you have the power to take action and grant yourself the wishes.

Can you do some research? Ask someone in that situation how they got there? Join a group? Read a book?

Ask for a change at work? Seek some coaching or support?

Wishes can come true if you're willing to make the effort to craft a step-by-step Map to your desires. Your ideal work life is nothing more than the fulfillment of a wish.

Other people do it, so why not you?

In the next section we are going to begin to put some structure around your dreams and put them in a container where we can sort through them and start to take action to make them real.

Right now, you may feel that you have a bunch of Clues but you're not sure how they go together?

Or if they do?

Or if they even need to? You may be feeling even more confused now, but don't worry. We aren't anywhere near the end of the process yet. The most important step is coming up.

What you need at this stage is Clarity.

Clarity

How Clear is Your Vision?

Clarity: the quality of being coherent and intelligible, OR the quality of transparency or purity – Merriam Webster Dictionary

Is your vision of your perfect work clear? Coherent? Pure?

I know that's probably a dumb question. This is probably the biggest hurdle of all of the 6 Tickets to Career Happiness Discovery.

Sure, it's hard to find the Courage, but you've braved tough things before.

And Clues can be a challenge if you are truly confused and don't know what to do.

After Clarity, we will talk about Community, and it can be difficult to infiltrate the right circles and find your people.

And the Compass is the actual Career Happiness Map, so there is some serious work in that section, although by then you'll be ready for it.

And Confidence is like the final entry ticket to your new life.

But Clarity? That's a bit of a pickle.

This is where the dreamy stage morphs into the reality phase. And sometimes reality can be a bubble buster.

But remember, through this whole process we are open-minded and thinking big. Playing it too safe keeps you stuck!

I can tell you from experience that when you get crystal clear on what you want, you can make it happen.

But you must put a voice to it.

Name What You Want

I earned my master's degree in Career Development in 2010. At the time I was a single mother of a teenager with debt, an expensive house, a car payment, and a lot of fear and doubt.

I saw no path in the near future that would lead me to the exciting world of career coaching, where I knew my passion and talents would be fully realized.

As my son grew into a man, and I married a new man and moved into his home, things started to shift for me. I felt freedom and options opening up.

Writing fiction created a tremendous confidence boost, as did singing karaoke in public, and things like traveling to Chicago alone to visit my son.

Slowly I started to feel what it would be like to quit my corporate job and start my own business.

At first it seemed like something far off – I would do it when I retired.

Then I said it would happen when my husband retired (he's 5 years older).

I kept moving up the timeline in my head as my desire and confidence swelled.

I started to imagine myself serving clients, creating programs, and writing this book!

In January 2019 I attended a retreat called Soulful Time Management led by a wonderful woman, Dr. Elaine Kiziah, who is now a mentor and friend.

Her retreat focused on journaling as a method to create what she calls a "beautiful life".

For me, career was my main focus because the other parts of my life were already pretty shiny.

This was such a life changing experience in the company of other wonderful, purposeful, spiritual women that we all asked Elaine to do a follow up session for us quarterly – so we wouldn't lose momentum on our progress.

You know how those new year's plans can go down

the drain fast?

Being an amazing woman, she organized a half day mini retreat in April. This time it was held at a co-working space here in Richmond called The Broad. It is a women-only organization (get it – The Broad? It's also on the corner of Broad St.) and I had no idea it existed.

I live out in the suburbs and The Broad is in the city, situated very inconspicuously - which is a good idea for the safety and privacy of its members.

The space is so beautiful and well designed. We sat in a room on pretty couches with amazing natural light streaming in the windows.

It felt like a home designed by a very stylish woman, yet it also felt like a place where important work was happening, and transformational connections were born.

Women were growing here. Contributing. Thriving.

Elaine informed me that she was a member of this club, and that she spent many days working in this space.

To say I was jealous was an understatement.

While we reconnected on the work we had done in January (which was so helpful!), I sat there drinking in the atmosphere, and as I walked around the top floor on our break and to journal in different corners of the space, I imagined myself working there.

Being a woman who runs her own successful business. Meeting people there. Creating. Communicating. A part of a tribe of women who also wanted more.

Fast forward to June 2019 I was officially a "Broad", and at the end of August I was a full-time entrepreneur.

No more juggling clients and content creation and social media posts with a day job.

I marked the end of doing work that didn't fill my spirit and my soul.

Recently I spent a Saturday at The Broad creating the invitations and flyers for my new group coaching program, Career Happiness Navigator, launching in January (along with this book!), and I was keenly aware of how happy I was to be there – not only in that space on the very couch I enjoyed a productive and inspirational afternoon with Elaine and the other "soulful" ladies, but there as in this career.

This life.

This is where gratitude is most important to attract more of what you want. And how did I begin to create the clarity around my career dreams, make them reality so quickly?

I named them.

I started to say out loud and to actual people (not just the dogs) that at some point (remember it started as a faraway plan) I was going to start a full-time career coaching business.

I declared it!

By doing that I cleared the space to attract this dream into my reality. The Universe didn't know I was serious until I called my dream by name.

Of course, I took inspired action to move forward, but it started with stating my intention out loud.

Nothing happens without intention.

And now I am bathed in gratitude when I remember the moments where I put myself first and dared to put a form and a name to my desires.

The memory of the feelings of my former self will continue to guide me along the path to more and better things in business and life.

Remember it's all connected!

But before we dive into a *new* idea, let's be sure you are running *to* something, and not *away* from something.

MUST You Quit Your Job?

Wouldn't it be amazing if you didn't have to quit your job in order to love it again? Or love it for the first time?

Now I know you may be thinking, "Carol, I thought you were all about career change and leaving bad work situations to pursue your Career Happiness? Isn't this the section on Clarity? We did all that work in the last section. Now you want us to stay where we are. Have you lost it?"

No, I promise I am still on top of it, and I want to ensure that you truly need to make an enormous change to get what you want – before you do the big work that's coming.

Remember, we are analyzing your situation from *all angles*, and we are breaking it down to its core and building it back up again.

At one time, did you love your job/work/career/business?

Look back at the Clues you came up with in the last section and apply them back to your current job reality.

You must dispel your previous limiting beliefs about your company/boss/field, etc. in order to do this properly. We are doing this work from a place of power and taking back control of our own careers and lives.

So, let's take a closer look at your current work.

Humor me – even if you mortally hate it, this exercise can create more Clarity around your ideal work and what steps you will need to take to manifest it.

Is your current job a place where you can make improvements? Even temporary ones while you pursue your dream career on the side?

Maybe it will take many steps to get to your ideal work and your Career Happiness Map is a long journey. Does that mean you should give up? Or that your only choice is suffer in the meantime, or quit and live in a trash can until your dream work appears?

Obviously not. You have many choices – you're just not seeing them. Keep your detective hat on, lady.

Here's an analogy you can probably relate to, whether or not you've had marital/relationship troubles. And if you haven't, YOU need to write a different kind of book!

Not all marriages that have gone south need to end in divorce. Marriage counseling does help some couples, as does better communication and a willingness to work together to achieve happiness.

Similarly, you don't *always* have to break up with your current employer in order to have the career you crave.

It does take some work to determine if this is even possible. I am not saying it *always* is but it's worth a shot, especially if you have invested a lot of time and energy into your job, it's a well-respected company, or you like your boss/co-workers/cafeteria/stock options, etc.

Sometimes we run from one bad work situation to another, without stopping to think about it from a career management standpoint.

Just like we shouldn't keep dating or marrying the same guy, even though his name changes – if being with him makes us feel unhappy.

Different isn't necessarily *better* when we are running *away* from something instead of running *towards* something that you've carefully crafted through serious thought and inner work.

Be honest with yourself. Remember, this work is for *you*.

Please get out your journal and write for a few minutes on this question - are you doing all you can to maximize what you already have in your current job?

If you suspect the answer may be no (and it often is), how do you fix that? How do you make the most of a bad situation? Get something back on track that has derailed?

Here is one very practical way, and it's something you already must do every year (usually twice a year), whether you want to or not.

In most organizations, you are asked to do a self-performance review. In my corporate experience, it is usually done twice a year, and is connected to your employer's review of your performance.

Yuck, right? I always hated doing those, even when things were good. But when things were not good, it was next to impossible!

But how about we look at it as an opportunity to ask for what we want? It's easy to let this process create stress and overwhelm.

- "What do they want me to say?"
- "Should I toot my own horn?"
- "Be a little self-deprecating?"
- "What if my boss is worried that I want his/her job?"
- "How can I say I'm unhappy without looking like an ungrateful jerk no one wants around?"

If you're anything like me and you tend to overanalyze all the things, you need to step back and think about why you are being asked to do this self-review exercise.

Your employer wants to know your thoughts because they want to discover if you are all on the same page. Your manager is not a mind reader and may have many direct reports and a lot of responsibilities that make career development an area that is sorely neglected.

This is why career coaching is so valuable – companies very rarely provide this service to their employees in any meaningful way.

And anyone who works for the organization is an agent of the company. They can't work for you the way an independent coach can.

This was one of my own Clues – I wanted to coach people with the person's highest good in mind – not the company's. I was unable to do this as a career coach in a corporate environment.

However, during my corporate years I learned a lot about the inner workings of the performance review process and I offer guidance here as to how to make it work for you, even if only as a Band-Aid on the road to your ultimate Career Happiness.

Remember, we are going on a journey, and we need to do *all* the steps to ensure the best, most fulfilling and exciting trip!

So, what can you do?

Let's say you'd like to learn about another department.

Say so.

Wish you could work on an interdepartmental project to gain new experience?

Tell your employer.

Would you like stretch assignments (work that is just outside of your main skill set designed to help you and the company grow and meet objectives)?

More travel? Less travel? The chance to implement a new idea you've been sitting on?

Help with navigating internal career opportunities to get promoted, or execute a lateral move to an area more suited to your career dreams?

More training and development opportunities?

Mentoring?

More flexibility?

ASK FOR THESE THINGS! SPEAK UP!

You get the picture. Hiding behind the damn Four Horsewomen of Bad Life Choices – (in case you forgot, they are fear, lack, judgment, and ignorance) will get you nowhere in the Clarity department.

Don't be afraid to ask for what you want. You are an adult and you have every right to ask for your needs to be met. You are not taking anyone hostage and making demands. You are keeping the organization's needs in mind. You know how you can contribute, and you want to!

Lack makes us feel like there isn't enough to go around. Even if you think the company doesn't have the ability to give you more money, freedom, training, etc. – it may not be true!

You won't know unless you ask. No one is going to come to you and offer you a cookie at nap time, like your teacher did in kindergarten. We must assert ourselves.

Don't judge a situation before you...wait for it...you

know what I'm going to say...

ASK!

And ignorance truly just means we don't know. Remember my son with the non-stop "whys"?

You don't have to act like a preschooler (and you're not as cute anymore!) to get information, but you don't know unless you:

ASK!

Sometimes, our managers assume we don't have any interest in change because we have never asked. Maybe she/he is waiting for you to come forward and show some initiative? Proof that you are engaged in your own career.

Before you decide that you can't have the career you want with your current employer, make sure that is really true. False limiting beliefs are one of the biggest causes of serial bad choices. That's how the Four Horsewomen stay alive. They feed on our inability to ask for what we want and to dig deeper into our dreams. To explore, to persist!

You may still find that after doing this exercise you do need to leave your job. I get it. Some bosses and organizations are just not going to meet us where we are and help us to move the needle on our dreams.

But don't jump from one bad job to another potentially unfulfilling workplace because you're not doing your part to manage your career, and make your needs, ideas, and aspirations known. Use the performance evaluation process to craft the job you want to have, and if that doesn't work:

Get out as fast as you can, and on the path to your Career Happiness!

However, you have nothing to lose and everything to gain - organizations that truly care about retaining and developing quality employees will welcome your enthusiastic and creative approach to this request for your input.

And those that don't - well, you'll know it and once you have that info, you're ready to launch your next career adventure.

If you do decide it's time to hit the road, where are you going?

Let's dig into another question that will provide Clarity for you on this journey to Career Happiness.

Yes, we are defining the crap out of your goals, but isn't it time?

Is It the Career Field, or the Job?

Now that you've taken some time to determine if your current role can be improved upon, or if it's time to leave your current job behind, let's dig even deeper.

Do you need a new *job*? Or a new *career*?

This is a vital turning point in the Career Happiness Discovery process.

Are you going to target other organizations where you can grow your current skillset in a similar role? Is it really the manager/co-workers/environment/industry/company culture?

OR do you need a full career pivot?

If it's a complete redesign you need, don't get sucked into thinking you just need another job doing the same work.

I did this for years in two distinct career fields – retail management (more on those dark days later) and recruiting.

Each time I thought I'd found a safe place to land. And while it is true that each time I changed jobs it was better; the improvement was short lived because I was not where I *truly* wanted to be.

I always felt like my true gifts and skills were being stifled, and I couldn't muster up the enthusiasm for the work that so many of my colleagues exhibited without any pain or effort.

There were Clues in all of that work that led me to where I am today, but they were also clear signs (Clarity) that I had an exit to reach that was way down the road, and I spent far too much time on this career road trip hanging out in sketchy rest areas with subpar restrooms and snack machines.

Be honest with yourself. Let go of the fear and worry about the future if you make a big change. Remember, no decision is irreversible, and you do not have to blink your eyes and adjust to a completely different life overnight. You don't really have a Genie in a bottle.

You have *you*, and the *tribe, teachers, and tools* I am going to help you to seek and utilize as you move step by step at YOUR pace along the journey.

But that's in the next section. Right now, we are still working on Clarity. So be clear and revisit your Less or More exercise.

Even if you had all the things in the More column, and you eliminated (or reduced) all of the items in the Less column, would you want your current job?

Would the WORK itself be satisfying? Or would it just be a little more tolerable?

If it's the latter, then perhaps you can use the performance review/communication route and make some positive changes in the short term, so things aren't so bleak and yucky while you are crafting your larger escape plan to a different field altogether.

If you love the WORK, but not the environment, and you've done everything you can to ASK for what you want in your current job, then you know that you need to launch a job search to another organization doing the same type of work.

My Career Happiness Navigator group coaching program delves deeply into the job search process, but that is beyond the scope of this book, which is focused on Career Happiness Discovery. In that 1:1 intensive program, we work to create the plan you will implement in your ultimate job search, just like we are doing together right now – only we talk...a lot. And I provide all the guidance and support you need to figure it out.

There are many stages and phases to do this process right, and to stop wasting time, money, and sleepless nights trying to figure it all out on your own.

However, even if you determine at this point in our time here together that you just need a new job, I still invite you to stick with me. The remaining tickets to Career Happiness Discovery – Community, Compass, and Confidence, are still very valuable for any job seeker.

And there is still more Clarity to be had as you continue to refine your goals and targets.

Before we hit a few more practical topics on our way out of this section (and they are a bit "tough love", just letting you know!), let's explore a common myth about work, and dispel more limiting beliefs around your goals and desires.

Does it seem like it would be difficult to blend your new targeted work into your life? Are you struggling with seeing your life as a whole, and your work as part of that complete system?

Is this happy work reality still feeling like it's a million miles away?

What if we reframe that whole concept?

The Work/Life Balance Myth

If you're close to my age (let's just say I've been in the workforce awhile), you've been hearing the term work life/balance for at least twenty or more years.

It's a great concept, right? But a bit of a tired expression. So many companies use this term only to pay lip service to its meaning, and they pretend that your "balance" is important.

Now of course there are some organizations who do this well, but the bottom line is - businesses exist to make money. Right? We can't fault them for that, and if they don't make money then you won't have a job.

So how do we find this elusive "balance" and still earn the money we need to have a great lifestyle?

For me, the secret has been doing what I love.

After many years of working in jobs I hated, I realized

something critical - in this work/life balance equation we are making the "work" part the *bad* part. The negative, yucky, "can't wait until it's over" part.

And we are trying to get more of what we *like*, which is what we refer to as the "life" part.

Does this mean we aren't living when we are at work??????

If so, that must stop RIGHT NOW!

While it is very enjoyable to spend time away from work because let's face it - we can't sit on a beach, go to the movies with our partners, or go dancing while working (and if you actually can do those things, I want to hear about THOSE jobs!), work CAN and SHOULD be fun!

Yes, I said it - FUN!

Whoever decided that work should be toil and misery, or drudgery and boredom, really SUCKS! This is an outdated social construct from a time when everything people did every day just to survive required endless labor and exhaustion.

We live in not only an industrial era, but an advanced technological time. We have many modern conveniences and tools to free up our time and provide us with a dizzying array of choices, if we are willing to see the buffet of career excitement that truly exists for EVERYONE!

Can we all do the same things? No. Are there *some* limits? Yes.

But chances are that the things you aren't good at are not the things you love anyway. And if you do aspire to do better at those weaker areas, you can always practice, take a class, and immerse yourself in study.

And if there is a skill you need to build to enjoy it more, it doesn't have to be your day job to add to your overall life satisfaction.

For now, just think about your limits and ask yourself – are they limits that matter in order to create your dream career into reality? And if not – they are not limits at all.

But if they are needed for your ideal work, figuring out how to improve in those areas is part of your Compass (AKA Career Happiness Map).

Even if you truly can't improve enough to use those skills at work, it's okay. The world needs the talents and skills of ALL people.

I don't feel badly that I could never be a doctor or an astronaut or a baseball player. There are plenty of people killing it in those fields, and today many of them are women. And they probably don't want to be coaches or speakers or authors. So, it's a win/win for all of us!

Therefore, let's dispel the work/life balance myth for the nonsense it is. You don't want balance – you want happiness. In whatever form that takes for you.

Let the Four Fairies of Infinite Possibility show you how to create a full life, one big part of which is your career.

Abundance, courage, curiosity, and knowledge are the ingredients to happiness. In all areas! You were meant to enjoy your life's work and to feel energized, fulfilled and at peace with your day to day contribution to the world.

It's a process, but one that can be fun and take less time than you think - but you must invest in your success in an intentional and actionable way.

It's time to love your WHOLE life!

Now a word of warning about another concept that can derail you on your quest for Career Happiness. Unfortunately, this one is disguised as a super positive and worthy practice.

But if you're not careful, it can lead you into a place of complacency and you'll find yourself with another big old stinking excuse.

Grateful NOT Satisfied

One of the most damaging limiting beliefs I have discovered has held me back for years – even when I was more than ready to make the leap into my current, beautiful, perfectly aligned work life:

I should be happy that I have a good job with benefits.

What a bunch of nonsense that is! I spent so much time focusing on my personal and spiritual development (all AMAZING work) that I started confusing gratitude with its jerky, evil twin – SETTLING!

I've kept a gratitude journal for the past ten years, and it is powerful and transformative. BUT – it's easy to fall into the trap that we should be so grateful for everything in our lives that we don't dare complain - because we know others have less. You can't receive more if you're not already happy with what you have.

Remember how grateful I am about working at The Broad and being a full-time career coach, and how I know that gratitude will help me grow my business?

So, we should always be grateful, right?

Well, yes...but also no. Being grateful for what you have is a good thing, but that doesn't mean you have to be grateful for *everything*, even the things that suck. *Especially* not the things that suck!

While it's a positive practice to count your blessings, and even look for them in something that you are unsatisfied with, that doesn't mean you need to hang onto it and not seek better.

That's like saying "well my husband doesn't cheat on me, so it's fine that he never talks to me or comes home".

Noooo!!!!

And I don't know about you, but the "eat your dinner because kids are going hungry in China" thing also doesn't work. Even as a child, you knew that eating your peas was not going to fill the bellies of anyone else in faraway lands. Are there ways to help the less fortunate? Of course! But the best way is when we have more for ourselves, so we have more to give.

There will always be someone with less of everything.

So, if we only strive to have more if we are in dire straits then we will never grow and develop. If we all just gave up and settled into what we have, no one would ever invent anything, create anything, or attempt anything!

Society would eventually cease to exist!

I have learned that I could be grateful for the jobs that I had, but still want to do more with my life. It was not only *okay to* want something different, but it was my *duty* to share my unique gifts with the world.

How about that? I am suggesting (strongly) that we are being *selfish* when we hide behind a gratitude practice to keep us from doing and being more.

So the next time you find yourself thinking that you should just be happy with what you have because it's more than others have – think about how much more you could help those others if you were the best, most prosperous, and fully embodied version of YOU!

Settling is nothing more than an excuse to stay stuck. And that's not allowed on the Career Happiness Discovery journey.

I Think You Know What You Want

I know you may argue with me on this one, but I think deep inside you know what you want. And if you didn't have a Clue when we started, you have lots of them now and you are working to piece them together into something that looks like a plan.

Sometimes we know what we want, but we overanalyze and let fear win. I desperately wanted to have my own career coaching business, and to write fiction in my house while most people are working in offices and commuting every day and dealing with bad bosses (I had some doozies!)

And I did move forward, even though my forward progression was more of a very squiggly line with lots of strife and struggle that could have been avoided – had I worked through this process systematically – like you're doing!

One of the biggest enemies of moving forward with your dreams is spending too much time on "research" and "getting ready" and "planning".

I know you're thinking that I shouldn't be advising you not to plan since this book is about discovering what you want to do and *making a plan* to get there.

Let me clarify (see what I did there in the section on Clarity?).

I love planning. It's exciting and feels motivational. However, it is easy to get stuck in that stage.

The sticky part is my concern for you, and that is why I move you swiftly along through this process. That's why my 1:1 Career Happiness Discovery coaching program is only 60 days and is designed to help you get fast action on TAKING ACTION!

In contrast, my Career Happiness Navigator program is a minimum of 3 months long, with the opportunity to stay enrolled as long as needed. It's a yearlong experience.

I am not assuming it will take you 3-6 months to find a new job – but I want you to stay in the ACTION part of the process for a longer period of time because you're making a major change and that can't happen overnight. You also need ongoing support as you transition to the change and prepare for the next step.

Career management is truly a lifelong personal development journey.

But the *starting* part needs to happen fast. If it doesn't you can waste months and years thinking and writing and researching and getting "set up".

Yes, it may take years to reach your ultimate goal – your *final* step on your Map. But it takes only this moment to begin. The road is long but once you're moving things begin to shift and evolve.

And as this happens, guess what? Things change again. And again. The Map you originally created in this process is a fluid document. As you gain more knowledge, meet more people, and have more experiences, your desires will shift. Doors will open, others will close.

Not only CAN you make changes and refine the goals along the way – you MUST. Your life is not a one and done process and remember – career is a huge, integrated PART of life. It is not a separate entity.

You *will* make adjustments so the most important thing to do is start. You can't implement nothing. Let's get it down on paper. We are going to use these notes to create your Map before we part company on this leg of your journey.

Problems are made to be solved, and do you know what makes you a good problem solver?

Solving problems.

Now, let's observe your new ideas through the lens of reality and tackle a couple of practical matters. Then we'll end this section with a topic I find quite eye opening.

Are You in the Right Place?

Are you in the right place?

For once I don't mean that in a metaphorical or philosophical sense.

I mean – do you live in an area/city that supports career opportunities in your chosen field?

I know when the word RELOCATION comes up, there can be a lot of emotions ignited for many people.

"Carol, I can't leave my family/friends/massage therapist/hairdresser/dentist/pet sitter, etc."

I understand it's harder if you have kids who are in school or a spouse with a full-time job.

However, PLENTY of people in these circumstances move far away to pursue their dreams.

What's it worth to you?

Are you just assuming you can't make it work? Or you won't be supported? Have you ever discussed this issue with your partner? Having a family and people who love you should be life enhancing, not life stifling.

Again, I am a mother and I know there are family responsibilities that make this a difficult hurdle for some people. Maybe it truly can't happen for you right now, in the way that would be best for your goals and dreams.

But I tell you what, sister – if it needs to happen some day in order to fully realize your potential as a human being, it needs to be addressed.

And in the meantime, creative solutions may need to be brainstormed as to how to move towards what you want from your current location. This is something a good coach can help you to sort out.

But assuming you don't fall into the small "I swear I absolutely can't relocate right now" category, are you using any of these assumptions as excuses to stay stuck?

If you long to be a marine biologist and you live in Kansas, or a TV star and you live in Alabama, or a cattle farmer and you live in Manhattan...

You get the idea.

And while those are extreme examples, there are places that are more conducive to success in one field or another. Some areas are heavy in defense, pharmaceuticals, entertainment, tourism, finance, fashion, etc.

You don't have to sell your house tomorrow and run out of town like your hair is on fire.

Just consider it. Are you in the right place to live your dreams?

It's part of the Clarity section because knowing where you need to *be* to live your career dreams is a vital practical piece of the Map.

After all, it's a *Map* and you're on it. You're not dangling somewhere in the cosmos.

I hope you will be honest with yourself. You've come so far in this process so don't quit on yourself now.

If the answer is no – start brainstorming on how you can find the ideal location to launch your passionate, happy career.

Or maybe your location is virtual – don't assume that's not an option for you. Let's explore.

And if you decide to jump into a different fishbowl, chances are the people in your life will swim there with you, and you can always find another wonderful massage therapist, hairdresser, dentist, and pet sitter.

I did. I moved from New York to Richmond, Virginia over 20 years ago with no job, a shaky marriage, and a four-year-old who had only been cared for by Grandma. We left our families and friends and knew absolutely no one in our new location.

I now feel confident that I could move anywhere and make a happy life because I don't let outside circumstances and limiting beliefs control me anymore.

My people are everywhere.

Opportunities are everywhere.

There are tons of good practitioners of every trade and craft that I can attract to fulfill all my needs at the highest level.

Remember you don't have to do it all at once to start. As with every part of this process, swift but measured *action* is the way to go. You're not running away; you are moving towards something you are creating.

Also, there is no need to speed there like a maniac – if you do that while driving you get into accidents or get a ticket. You want to get there – not burn out and make impulsive decisions.

Purposeful planning and inspired action.

Now, here's another favorite excuse of many people who are stuck in the wrong career. It's riddled with dream crushing beliefs that are almost always untrue.

Get ready to learn something about learning.

A Student of Life

Client: "Carol, I can't go back to school! I'll be 40, 50, 60 by the time I graduate!"

Me: "Well, if you don't go back to school, won't you still be 40, 50, 60?"

Client: "Of course."

Me: "Wouldn't you rather be 40, 50, 60 with a degree in a field that can help you to pursue your goals, or give you the knowledge and tools to enjoy your work and your life?"

Client: "When you put it like that, I guess I should go back to school. You're a genius, Carol! Everyone should work with you!"

I threw in the last sentence for fun, but you get the picture.

I am not suggesting that *everyone* should go back to school at any age. What I am insisting is that if you have a burning desire to further educate yourself, you should not let your age stop you.

As long as you are healthy in mind and body, there is no age at which it's okay to just give up.

Sure, you may not have the same 30 or 40 years to enjoy this new career the way you would have if you had chosen this path at age 20.

But so what? That was then and this is now, woman. So school is NOT off the table. Whether it's a degree program, a certificate, a workshop - it doesn't matter. Learning keeps us young and inspires us to do great things.

What would you like to learn? I bet some possibilities came up for you as you started refining your goals in this section. I hope you didn't throw those ideas out the window because they require more education.

Or you suspect that they do. This is also sometimes untrue and there are other ways to break into your ideal work. Dig deep before you decide you know everything and have permission to give up! As you know by now, I won't let you off the hook that easily.

Or maybe ever.

I earned my master's degree in career development at 42. And if there was another degree I felt would help me reach a new goal, I wouldn't hesitate to sign up.

Live your WHOLE life - not just the young part. Cutting off our options as we age is one of the causes of feeling old. Before you decide that people your age can't or shouldn't do something, change your thinking!

You know how someone your age can do things?

By doing them!

The rejection of education as an option, and the limiting belief that it's too late to start over, comes up for my clients often – even some who are only in their late 20's!

This one pains me the most because why would we ever think that there is an expiration date on happiness and self-development? Did you wake up today? Then it's not too late. Don't stop living your life while your heart is still beating!

Here is a quick story of one woman who is bravely stepping over this fear and living her one life to the fullest.

I recently had the privilege of doing some laser coaching (short, private sessions on a specific career issue) at a women's professional conference and met an amazing woman who is leaving a long career in accounting and going to medical school! She is 51 years young!! I just wanted to hug her!

When I asked her why she chose a finance career as opposed to pursuing her medical dreams when she went to college as a young girl, she shared that a counselor advised her to avoid the medical field because "black people don't do well in health fields".

When I recovered from my shock and disgust, she asked me if I thought she was crazy, and that many of her friends and family have told her it's too late. I encouraged her to avoid discussing this dream with those people until it is well under way, and to keep her goals close while she builds her confidence and puts her plan in motion.

I was soooo proud of this brave woman – she could have easily let that horrible, racist, ignorant person ruin her whole life. But she's finally found the courage to live her dream! Who cares that she won't be a practicing physician until she's in her late 50's? She told me that she will enjoy the whole journey. Wow!

What stories were you told that have kept you back? It's time to let them go!!

What could you study and learn that would help you enjoy your *whole* life?

Career Happiness Medley

We need to make choices, but must it be all or nothing?

I spent years mired in the "I don't know what I want" place, even though I damn well did know – I just didn't see a path to getting there, AND I wanted more than one thing.

What????

I didn't know it was okay to feel that way until I met Barbara Sher. Well, I didn't *meet* her – I read her books. Her work in career development circles is legendary and I devoured all her words.

She calls people who "Refuse to Choose", Scanners.

Over the years, others have written books on this topic and called the multi-passionate career seekers by many different names.

But one name that is common for all of them at one point or another is – Confused.

Most of us were taught that you pick a career and put all your efforts into that one thing and move up and get ahead and retire with a pension and a gold watch.

It's difficult for most of us to even imagine that scenario anymore. The world has changed so much that it's likely that your parents didn't even follow that path, depending on your age and how adventurous your family leans.

If you wanted to do other things, there were called hobbies. And most people feel like they don't have time to pursue them, especially while raising a family.

When I was in my late 30's, I had been divorced for a few years and I was a single mother of a young teenaged boy. My burning desire for more was taking over, and now that I had no partner who could stop me from pursuing my dreams (yes, I agree that he didn't really *stop* me but the wrong relationships can thwart our efforts – more on that in the Community section coming up), I was ready to jump into…something.

I had about 8 or 9 years of recruiting experience at that time, and while I loved working with candidates in their job searches, I was never an agent of the job seeker, and I wanted to be. I yearned to help people with their careers and guide them down the path to their ideal work.

I researched all sorts of programs and decided to enroll in John F. Kennedy University's Career Development master's degree program (that program no longer exists, which makes me sad!).

JFKU is located in the San Francisco Bay area and I live in Virginia. But it was 2007 and many programs were going virtual with online components. I only had to commit to going to California for two summers, for one week of intensive onsite learning each visit.

My son was 13 and his father was very involved in his life, so going away without him wasn't an issue. I had no obstacles, only the little voice that creates doubt.

One of the requirements of acceptance into the program was a conversation with the Program Director. It wasn't so much an interview, but a reality check and "level setting expectations" exercise.

It was important to me to get all my questions answered, and important to the Director to ensure she was bringing people into the program who would be successful.

I was walking in my neighborhood one hot summer day and she called. I accepted the call because I had been eagerly awaiting it, even though it was a Saturday.

Gail and I chatted about the program and my goals. I was concerned about the logistics and wanted to be assured that the distance wasn't going to diminish my learning experience.

One thing Gail told me that stood out was – the most successful career development professionals have "portfolio careers".

I had never heard of this term but when I realized she was referring to Scanners, I understood. I can't recall exactly what different endeavors made up Gail's "portfolio" career at the time, but it was something like – "I teach at the University and run this program, and I do private career coaching, and I write articles and I do workshops at a local non-profit".

I had not heard of work so glamorous since I was the Silly Girl in the City.

What a wild experience to talk to someone who was living the "Refuse to Choose" concept and who was making a living by doing more than one job!

I had some knowledge of professional part-time work from my recruiting experience, and I had also done quite a bit of research into working mothers and how they were coping with the "Mommy Track", which was a term coined in the late eighties to describe the career path of mothers and how it couldn't possibly be the same as non-mothers or men.

That's another topic entirely, and in 2007 I was a mother whose child was marching towards independence, even though we had a number of years before he was ready to launch into the working world.

Gail asked me if I could see myself doing this work and living this life.

I said yes immediately, even though I knew I would not be able to realistically figure out how to do it right away. I needed a stable job, and I was well paid by my corporate employer.

But I knew it would take me a few years taking classes part-time to complete the degree, and I was willing to bet that my circumstances would change by then.

This piece wasn't well thought out at the time, but I knew with great certainty that this was work I was meant to do, and I would figure out how to make it happen.

On to the next hurdle. Money. I didn't think my company would approve this degree for tuition reimbursement because it wasn't directly related to their work.

But, guess what? I asked and they did.

And guess what else? After I finished the program, they allowed me to offer career coaching services to employees.

I also asked for that.

My father, who spent his entire career in sales, used to tell me, "No is painless."

And it's true. It only causes pain because we take it personally. We allow others to define us and lower our worth.

But risking rejection is part of everything we do that's worth doing.

Later on, after meeting my current husband and allowing my dream of a private career coaching practice to remain on hold until my son was independent, I began another journey.

I had wanted to write books since I could read them. I let that dream die and become deeply buried for my entire teen and adult years.

At 45, I started writing a book in secret. I wasn't sure if I wanted anyone to read it. I was terrified of rejection and didn't see how I would make the time to complete the project with my full work and social schedule, as well as my son and home to take care of.

But I did it. And in the past 6 years I have published 8 novels, 2 short story collections, and this book.

During that time, I also planned a wedding, launched a child into a successful college and working life, and moved out of my house into my new husband's house.

You can do all the things you desire. Just don't let the fear of "no" get in your way, or any obstacle that tells you it's too hard, it's too late, or any other crap that keeps you from living your full expression.

Having like-minded, supportive people on the journey

helps a lot, and that was an area where I was sorely lacking. I had to become my own supportive person, but that isn't necessary for you.

Or me – I just didn't see it at the time. There is no need to go it alone when your people are out there.

Now that you know where you'd like to end up, and some ideas about how you might get there, let's talk a bit (or a LOT) about how you can surround yourself with the ongoing support, knowledge, and resources to keep going, even when the going gets tough.

On a long road trip, it's always more fun when you have friends along. And some snacks and breaks, and the GPS is working.

Let's surround you with what you need to keep going – your tribe, teachers and tools!

Community

Where Are Your People?

Community: a feeling of fellowship with others, as a result of sharing common attitudes, interests and goals – Merriam Webster Dictionary

Who do you spend your time with? Does it feel like a fellowship? A sisterhood? Do you share common attitudes, interests, and goals?

When I made a commitment to myself to embark on this entrepreneurial journey, I realized that most of the people I spent time with did not share my attitudes, interests, and goals. As a matter of fact, a year or more ago I would have been hard pressed to name more than a couple of people I could talk to about my plans, or even who enjoyed the same music as me!

One of the things I knew I had to do in order to be successful was to actively seek out the tribe, teachers, and tools that would create a community framework from which I could launch my dreams.

None of us exist alone, and while being independent is a wonderful way to be (and very necessary in order to find the confidence to make major changes), we all need to find the people and resources to support us in all areas of life.

We truly are better together. There is power in Community – especially in communities of like-minded women.

So, where are these people? How did I find them? How is it that my circle has grown and changed dramatically in less than a year – to the point where I no longer recognize my life – in a good way?

Now that you're gained the Courage to begin, you've gather the Clues to find your goal, and you've put some Clarity around it, let's talk about building the Community that will help you create and implement your dream work.

The New Networking

When I think of networking, I think of a bunch of people in suits, holding drinks, wearing name tags, and having boring conversations.

Yuck, right?

"But we need to network, Carol! Isn't that what this section is all about?"

Yes, you do! And yes, it is! But, let's not call it that.

What we need to do is CONNECT.

Connection takes many forms. We connect with people every day. We engage with the world, both online and in person. We have SO many opportunities to do this in our world today. It's truly endless, no matter what your interests!

So, instead of just going to a professional association meeting, or events offered by your current employer, consider joining something new.

- It could be a Meetup group, a Facebook community, an online group that shares your interests, or your struggles.
- You could volunteer for a cause that matters to you.
- Take a class.
- Join a club.
- Play a sport.
- Mingle after your worship service.
- Attend your community meetings.
- Go to the pool in your neighborhood.

If you're more introverted, concentrate on online groups or find a bunch of other introverts and hang out with them. Find Community on *your* terms.

The possibilities are endless. The more new people you can truly CONNECT with, the more you will learn about yourself and where your passions lie. We see ourselves in others – they act as a mirror and they teach us more about who and what we want to be.

Nothing changes if nothing changes. So, consider changing where, when and who you spend time with.

You don't have to abandon everyone currently in your life. In fact, that would be an awful thing to do – unless you are truly part of a toxic tribe, and if so, go back to the section on relocation!

Just mix it up. Explore the richness of the diversity of this world. Even your little corner of it. Adventure…and answers await.

I have joined numerous women's circles for both personal and professional growth. Each one is a little different. Some are more diverse, and others are filled with members who are more like me.

However, every one of them has the following commonalities – they are all supportive and fun sisterhoods dedicated to growth, success, and happiness.

Your tribe is all around you, no matter where you live. It's time to shake things up and let your judgment fly out the window (one of the icky Four Horsewomen of Bad Life Decisions) and open yourself up to new people, places, and things.

Now, let's briefly look at your tribe of origin and how it has affected you. Sometimes we need to go back for a minute to move forward.

Role Models: Positive Example or Tragic Warning?

Who taught you about work? Who were your work role models?

Did they work hard? Were they a bit lazy?

How about their attitude towards money? Did they work harder to make more? Did they prefer to save every dime, so they didn't have to work harder? Or make changes?

Was work more about service to others than making money? Was there greed involved?

Did your role models struggle to find work, keep work, or succeed at work? Or were they super successful and intimidating?

Take some time to examine where your beliefs about work come from. Are they positive or negative? Helping or hurting? Do they serve you now?

That's the most important question.

Don't spend a ton of time on this exercise. Don't DWELL on anything negative or yucky or uncomfortable that arises. We want to understand the past so that we can plant positive seeds for future growth, but we don't want to wallow there or use any of our past experiences as *excuses*.

Once you have it figured out, just release what doesn't work, what doesn't really BELONG to you, and what may be holding you back. And bless it and let it go.

Write it on a piece of paper and burn it. Bury it in the backyard. Put it through the shredder. Toss it in the river. Just get rid of it!

Most of the time people in our lives mean well. They tried. They were figuring out their own path and they had their own struggles. You may not even know about the root of their fears or pain or confusion – especially your parents and other adults in your life when you were a child. They did not share all their stuff with you, but you absorbed it through teaching and example.

But none of that is *yours*.

Free up that mental space to bring in new beliefs of hope and possibility and abundance. I promise you'll feel lighter, and ready to design a career that is YOURS!

I am not a therapist, and this book is not to be used as a replacement for that kind of help. If things come up for you in this process that feel heavy, and they derail you from this work, put this book down and get the help you need to make peace with the past.

But if you can examine these questions (ideally in your journal!) and you can clearly see how past beliefs are false for you, let them go and allow yourself the space for new ideas, people and experiences to come into your life.

We always have the power to change our thoughts and beliefs. While we all must deal with outside circumstances and things that happen to us, we are the authors of our own stories.

Many times when I tell someone that I'm an author they say things like, "That's amazing, I could never write a book."

But you are writing one every day, and the people in your life, especially the younger ones, are influenced by *your* story. When we live intentionally, not only do we bring what we want into our world, we add to the greater world in a meaningful way.

Isn't that a cool definition of Community?

It's one where we have way more power than we think to create our own reality.

Now that you've had some time to reflect on the past, let's jump back to the present and figure out who can stay and who can go – as you get ready to set off on this path to your ideal work and life.

Is Your Tribe Toxic?

Let's talk about the people in your life.

Yes, we are doing this again. It's that important.

Toxic people suck. Yes, I am getting right down to it without any flowery lead in. In order to find your Career (and Life) Happiness you need to surround yourself with positive people who support you and lift you up.

The good news is - they don't have to be exactly like you, or even completely understand your goals. They just have to be on your side. In your corner. Rooting for you.

I have held onto many relationships in my life where the other person was draining my energy, making me feel bad about myself, or simply not participating in a "relationship" - meaning a real give and take of ideas, interests, empathy, and support.

And worst of all, there was no FUN!

Just as I believe work can and should be fun, our relationships with other humans must also be fun!

If you are going to embark on a mid-career change, you must surround yourself with light and love, not darkness and any negative emotion that drags you down.

I invite you to assess who you are spending your time with and why. There are billions of people in the world. Your ideal tribe is out there. And who knows - maybe some of them can help lead you to your ideal work.

Many of us live our lives for the people we know and love, and not for ourselves and our highest good. We worry about what people will think if we choose to make major changes. It's easy to fall into the trap of living for other people - for their hopes and dreams and expectations of you. It starts out with parents, teachers, and friends. Then it moves to co-workers, partners, and even our own kids!

We all like it when people think highly of us and when we are accepted, right?

Yes, that is human nature because we are born social creatures. We need other people, but...

What are you *losing* by living for someone else's view of your life? Why are you giving them that power? If they abandon you because you make a change that isn't in line with their view of you, were they ever really a genuine positive person in your life?

Often the issue is that people are threatened when we change because it sheds a light on their inaction, their fears, etc. And they project all that yucky crap onto us.

- "That's a crazy idea."
- "You'll never be able to do that?"
- "Can't you just be happy with what you have?"
- "Who do you think you are?"

Answers:

- "I love my idea."
- "Yes, I will!"
- "No, I can't. I want more."
- "I think I am a valuable, unique individual who has the right and duty to share her authentic gifts with the world."

We have enough of our own stuff to sift through, and the last thing we need is carrying the burden of other people's unresolved baggage and false beliefs.

I invite you to open your journal and examine your fears surrounding others' judgment of you, and decide - is this my issue or someone else's? Is this belief real or true? Sometimes we are so deeply ingrained in our programming that we aren't sure anymore where we end, and others begin.

Reframing your attitude and reaction to the opinions of others is a powerful exercise in getting unstuck in your career...and your life.

It's all intertwined!

I understand that some of the toxic people may be your loved ones, and that makes this a painful exercise. Again, I am not a therapist and if those close relationships are the ones holding you back, perhaps you need more than this book, or any book, can provide to help you move the needle on your dreams. I am merely a guide and this book seeks to empower you to uncover your path – and part of that is clearing the way. You can't drive on a road filled with debris and obstacles.

Removing toxic people from your life can be a gradual process or weaning yourself off these relationships.

You may even find that as you add new people, you are not so dependent on the current circle to fulfill your needs, and you can enjoy them more, despite their limitations.

But sometimes someone is such a negative, draining influence on your life that you need to drop them like a hot potato. You can't drive down the road to Career Happiness with burned hands!

Community is an area that takes some time to develop. It doesn't happen overnight. However, if you make an intentional effort to connect with new people, you will be amazed at how quickly your life will transform.

A new tribe will bring new teachers who will share with you new tools, and you will see new doors opening – ones you didn't even know were there or available to you.

But you must seek them out. Knock on them. There is a whole new world waiting on the other side.

You're about to plan your trip now – isn't that exciting?

Before we start the Compass section, don't forget that you don't have to know everything in order to start. Let go of your critical, worried voice – the one who tells you that your plan is unrealistic or not well defined enough, or crazy, etc.

Instead of concerning yourself with *how* you will reach the end goals *all at once* (that's most likely impossible), let's look at how you can break it down into steps.

Even baby steps.

This is *your* Map, and it can be designed to suit your unique needs, temperament, and pace. You don't need to speed up or slow down.

The whole point of the entire Career Happiness Discovery process is that you are in the driver's seat. It's about reclaiming control and power – and being authentically you.

The only rule is to move forward and take action. Inspired action – not erratic movement fueled by outside circumstances.

You are not a passenger on this journey. You are the trailblazer! So, let's begin to set the course for your exciting new career adventure!

Compass

Asking for Directions

Compass: an instrument containing a magnetized pointer which shows the direction of magnetic north and bearings from it – Merriam Webster Dictionary

If you're old enough to have traveled before GPS technology, then you remember what fun it was to ask for directions on a trip.

Of course, none of us are old enough to remember walking through the woods with only a Compass to guide us, although I'm guessing this might be something still taught in Boy or Girl Scouts, or some other wilderness adventure club I know nothing about.

I was never the best map reader and I also have motion sickness, so trying to read the map while someone else drives is hard for me. My ex-husband used to get upset with me for giving poor navigation, and like most men he hated to admit that stopping at a gas station to ask for directions was necessary if we ever wanted to reach our destination.

I frequently went inside and asked for directions, because he was also shy, and I had less of a problem talking to strangers. However, the person on the other side of the counter was in fact a stranger, and I had zero idea if this person was going to point us in the right direction or send us miles off course. And if I didn't write it down, I was lost after the second turn they rattled off.

These were wild times, and I can't believe how easy it is to travel now. The route is always programmed, and we just move through the steps. The GPS even tells us when there is traffic or an accident or a road closure.

We are going to work on your Career Happiness Map, but unlike the cartographers of old, we are going to program yours into a navigation system that will empower you to anticipate changes, make the necessary adjustments, and stop and rest when you're too tired to keep going.

This is your dream trip and you are in charge. You will ask for help along the way, but not blindly. If the person on the other side of the counter gives you wrong information, you don't have to accept it at face value. You can research the info, ask for a second opinion, and test the waters.

You have access to a never-ending amount of information, all at your fingertips. The tools exist for you to learn and grow like never before. There is no need to go miles out of the way before you course correct, and you are not bound by time either. This is your journey and whether or not it's a weekend getaway or a sabbatical of several years, is up to you.

You don't need to get sick looking at the Map while you're driving, and you don't need to argue with anyone else about the path, the next turn, or when it's time to find a rest stop because you really have to pee (this is a huge problem for me, haha).

The name of this game is Mindful and Flexible Planning.

You know where you are going and why, but you're not so rigid that there is no room for detours. It may be a cheesy cliché, but life is a journey, not a destination. You may stop for long periods of time in one place, but you can always move on, too.

It's all in your capable hands.

At the end of this section, I am going to invite you to begin putting your Career Happiness Map down on paper. Only the first 1-3 steps need to be actionable and realistic in the beginning.

Remember, as you travel things will change. And that's okay. This Map is written in pencil and you always have the eraser with you.

Planning Gets a Bad Rap

I find that most people fall in one of two categories when it comes to planning – those who plan everything, and those who resist structure in their lives.

I am a planning addict. Yes, I said it. But I have no intentions of trying to recover – in fact, I am digging even more deeply into planning to reach my goals. However, it is intentional planning now. Actionable planning.

How is that different than regular planning? Isn't planning just writing down the stuff you're going to do and keeping to-do lists?

Not really, but we'll get to that in a minute. First let's talk about the rebels.

You know who you are.

Many people see the idea of planning as restrictive. If they plan all their time, how will they leave room for spontaneity? They fear that if they plan too much or too far in advance, they won't be able to accept exciting last-minute invitations or take advantage of opportunities as they arise.

And worst of all, they don't know if they will feel like experiencing planned activities on the days they fall on the calendar. Can't we just go with the flow?

No, you really can't. Not if you want to implement major changes over time.

If you don't plan, you have no direction. A road trip with no plan can be fun and adventurous if it's a vacation from your already amazing career/life – but if we are talking about making significant changes in your career and your day to day existence, we need to work on that a bit more mindfully.

Can you factor in breaks and free time to allow the "flow" to enter? Sure, but if all you have is "flow", you're not in charge. The river flows of its own power, not yours.

The trick is to make the plan work for you – not let

the plan control you. If you're the one making the plan, then it's not restrictive – it's full of things YOU want to do and achieve.

Have you ever discovered that your favorite band was coming to your town on their concert tour, but the tickets went on sale many months in advance?

And were you super excited, but when it came time to buy them you hesitated because you didn't know if you'd be able to go when the day came around?

And did you decide to wait to buy them? Maybe you even forgot all about it until someone posted on Facebook about how excited they were that they had tickets to the show?

And then did you try to get your tickets and the show was sold out or only the worst and/or most expensive tickets were left?

I have missed out on many shows when I have left it to someone else to secure my ticket. If I see something I want to do, I immediately jump on it and get tickets.

When I was single, I would sometimes even do it without knowing who was coming with me. I will not let the indecision or limitations of others keep me from what I want.

The same holds true for hotel and plane reservations, dinner at a favorite restaurant on a holiday, or buying something that's on sale for a limited time.

Saying yes quickly can mean the difference between having an amazing, life changing experience or staying stuck in the same place.

Planning is vital to career success. You can't even write your resume if you don't know what jobs you are targeting. Well, you technically *can*, but you'll never get the job you want.

Don't let your rebellious nature be an excuse for laziness and procrastination.

Now, just so you don't think I am biased towards the super planners, I will address my sisters in structure with some words of caution.

Be careful that you don't spend so much time planning that you never actually *do* anything.

Sometimes we get so caught up in the plan, that we never take any action.

When I outline a novel, I can get so caught up in knowing how every piece is going to unfold that I am afraid to start writing. I've learned that I need a loose outline but that the story will always change and evolve as I write it – just like my life and career path.

Planning is not a one and done activity, and it is also not *action*. It's preparing for action.

The main thing planning does for us is to serve as a guide – an intentional Map that is moving us in the right direction. But you must actually *move*.

I can spend hours writing and rewriting lists and scheduling time in my calendar. And then I catch myself. Does it really matter what I'm going to be doing on Tuesdays in May of next year, when it's Halloween of the previous year?

Not really. It's fine to have an *idea*, but there is a reason I write everything in pencil, and I use the Trello app to track projects.

Everything changes.

But we must start somewhere. I suggest a rough outline of what you'd like your career to look like in the next 1-3 years. Then start plotting the steps you need to take to get there. One at a time. Knowing that you will make adjustments along the way.

But don't be afraid to register for that class that doesn't start for six months, reserve your place in that group coaching program, buy that online course while it's on sale.

Don't miss out because you resist planning. Or you're not totally sure.

Go to the show, make reservations for New Year's Eve, and get the hotel room with the ocean view before it's scooped up.

Nothing happens unless you move forward – and

whether that's treading water in the river of indecisive rebellion, or swimming in circles in a lake full of lists, the end result is the same.

You stay stuck where you are.

Planning isn't controlling because you are the planner. The doer! It's time to bring those dreams we started with at the beginning of this journey to the doing stage.

Now let's review a couple of other stumbling blocks on the road to Career Happiness, and how they inhibit our process with their limitations.

Then I promise we will get more nitty gritty again and get into my 6 Tickets to Career Happiness Navigation (aka a successful job search).

Where Did the Time Go?

"Carol, I'd love to get unstuck and make a plan, but there's never enough time!"

I totally get this issue! I've been a working mother of a baby, a single mother of a school age to high school boy, I've juggled side hustles, fiction writing, and a myriad of hobbies and social commitments! All while trying to find my Career, and Life, Happiness!

Nothing annoys me more than a career/life guide that tells you all the things you need to do without any consideration for all the interruptions of daily life. As women, we are especially pulled in a million directions. Whether it's partners, kids, parents, friends, work, household chores, pets, health issues, or the ever-elusive self-care and exercise we all aspire to do but can't seem to fit in - we have a lot of demands on our time!

And we are all given the same number of hours in a day. However, I will invite you to take a closer look at *how* you spend your time (remember the planning discussion?).

Is it INTENTIONAL? Is it PROACTIVE? Is it in line with your hopes and dreams? Your plans and goals?

If it's not, you might want to take a step back and do

a little self-reflective journaling.

Go somewhere quiet, even if you must leave the house - just pretend you have a gynecologist appointment - no one in your house will want to discuss that.

Seriously - give yourself a little gift of time to reflect.

- Where are you wasting time with no return on investment of joy or success?
- Where can you ask for help?
- What can you outsource?
- Are the people in your life supporting your intentional use of your time?
- What myths are you believing about time?

Commit to making one change, even if it's a tiny shift. Sometimes changing one thing can be the start of changing many things, including your work life.

Getting unstuck in your career isn't always directly about working on a job search, or even immediately identifying what you want to pursue. It starts with movement, which leads to change and growth.

How can you restructure the way you spend your precious time to enhance your precious life?

Is it necessary to do everything the way you currently do it? It's very easy to get into the habit of living a certain way and telling ourselves that's the only way it can be.

I am not a morning person. I have resisted getting up early my whole life. When I was younger, I supposed that would change as I got older - after all my parents and grandparents had no trouble getting up early!

In fact, it seemed the older the person, the earlier they woke up. My grandfather could be found fully dressed in the kitchen reading the newspaper at 4 in the morning!

And while I am not a grandmother yet, I am surely old enough that I am "older" from the viewpoint of my young self. And I still love to sleep late.

Working from home in my corporate jobs for the past

10 years allowed me to sleep much later than my commuting counterparts, and now that I'm a full-time entrepreneur I have the freedom to do whatever I want.

Thank goodness I have dogs – otherwise who knows how late I'd stay in bed.

I've been reading a lot about the benefits of waking up early and starting the day in a mindful way. My Inner Rebel has resisted this and made excuses about why it doesn't work for me, and I will be less productive because I will feel tired all day and I feel terrible when I wake up early, and I can just work later, etc.

Aren't excuses so easy to find? They're everywhere so you must be vigilant about swatting them away like flies at a picnic.

So last week I decided that I was going to get up 1.5 hours earlier than I normally do. I am not going to tell you what time that is because you will roll your eyes hard and/or decide that my advice is worthless. My early time is still a time when many people are already at work, or at least driving.

Long story short, I did it. I got up early every day. And one of the days I got up 2 hours early because I have a professional association meeting once a month that starts at a time when I usually wouldn't be awake and/or able to talk to people, not even my husband.

I have been blown away with the level of productivity I have been able to achieve in those early morning hours, and throughout the day. My output has been off the charts.

And the best part is that I don't feel any more tired than I normally do during the day, or even at bedtime.

Therefore, I never needed that much sleep. It was a limiting belief I have been telling myself for years. I would even go so far as to say that I was clinging to this view of how I spend my time as a defense mechanism for why I can't be successful.

Wow!

Sure, it sucks to wake up when I want to keep sleeping, but it only feels bad for the first five minutes after I'm awake. Once I begin the day and become engaged in all the fun and exciting projects I have *planned* for the day, I'm alert and productive.

And when noon rolls around I feel like I've already completed a whole day's work.

I can't believe I didn't realize this sooner.

Hmm, what else can we reframe?

The Gift of Failures

It's too scary!! What if I fail??

We've all experienced this feeling at one time or another, and it's real!

However, I will invite you to consider that avoiding action because you are afraid of failure means that you are only succeeding at doing nothing, or at the very least - you are stuck in a career ditch and can't figure out how to dig your way out.

OR maybe you KNOW what to do, but this fear is holding you back?

It's usually the latter. In getting unstuck, it helps to dig deeper into the "WHY" of what we do, and don't do.

- What were you taught about failure?
- Why are you so afraid to make mistakes?
- What will happen if you do the thing you long to do, but you aren't immediately successful?
- Why is it so terrible if you have to work at it?
- Change course?
- Learn from your mistakes?
- Who are you trying to please?
- Are you living for someone else's view of what your career and life should look like?

These are hard questions, and I know they're a bit of

tough love. Please take some time to journal on these, either now or come back to this exercise when you're ready for this part of the process.

We must hold ourselves accountable and uncover where we are holding our own dreams hostage. No one who is successful at anything got there by playing it safe, by hiding from the possibility of failure. Truly the only failure is doing nothing to improve your life.

I blame our school systems on reinforcing this idea of failure. If you fail a test, you can't retake it. There is no opportunity to improve, which would foster actual learning and growth, instead of just measuring your ability to memorize and regurgitate information at one moment in time.

But I could write a whole book on my opinions on education, even though it's not my area of professional expertise. Although I would argue all day long that the way we educate our children has a lot to do with their future career success and life happiness.

But for most of us, we must reprogram ourselves – no one is going to do it for us, and blaming the past is just another big fat stinking excuse.

So, what is one thing you could do today to overcome your fear of failure? What's one baby step? You don't have to leap across the canyon over a pit of snakes.

Or whatever your equivalent horrifying scenario would be.

Just do one thing to loosen up this fear and prove it wrong.

If you're not failing, you aren't doing anything. You certainly aren't stretching or challenging yourself.

And how do you know how far you can go if you don't try? If you don't push against the boundaries of your abilities?

Failure allows us to learn about what doesn't work and to do that all-important refining and course correcting. The truth is we don't know if something is going to work before we try it, especially if it's something new for us.

Instead of worrying about failing, how about we focus on making mistakes as a path to finding the right way to do things – the way that will lead us to our own brand of happiness.

Because the more important and transformational question is - what will your life look like if you succeed?

Failure only hurts if you give it the power to harm you. Instead, turn it around and let it be your greatest teacher. And remember, don't worry about other people – if they aren't failing it's because they aren't doing jack squat to change their lives for the better.

And you are killing it!

Now that we've addressed the issues that may hold you back from creating your Map, I'd like to invite you to take some time to sketch a rough draft of the path you'd like to follow to reach your career goal.

Use the knowledge gained through your journaling exercises (you've been doing those right?).

If not, it's okay - just read the book again and pause at the questions for written self-reflection and begin to build the foundation upon which your career dreams will grow and develop into reality.

I'll wait.

If you have been actively working through the process as you move through this book, we are ready to talk about your job search/map implementation.

Depending on the steps of your Map, you may need to do one or many steps before you are ready to seek the opportunity that will fulfill your goals.

But even if that's the case, the next short section will give you an overview of how to prepare for the most practical piece of this journey.

Details about job searching mechanics are beyond the scope of this book but are covered in-depth in my Career Happiness Navigator group coaching program.

For women who are serious about making their career

dreams real, this 3-6-month program guides Career Happiness Seekers through the job search and beyond into career management tools for lifelong career satisfaction.

For now, let's touch on the job search piece, because when you close this book and begin your journey, I want you to have some guidance to start manifesting what you've outlined in this Career Happiness Discovery process.

Remember, I'm all about action!

The 6 Tickets to a Successful Job Search

- **Content** – design job search materials that attract attention
- **Connection** – form a tribe of supportive mentors and real job leads
- **Communication** – learn how to present your very best self
- **Compensation** – negotiate your worth and earn more money
- **Culture** – discover and locate your ideal work environment
- **Cruise** – strategize your career plan to excel and advance in your new job

"Carol, why do all your "Tickets" start with a "C"? And why "Tickets?"

I ask myself these kinds of questions all the time. I think the use of the letter "C" ties into both my name and the word "career". I didn't plan that (hahaha, so not everything is planned), but I think my subconscious led me down that path.

And Tickets are things we need to gain entry to desired activities. Without them we sit on the sidelines and watch other people have all the fun, satisfaction, and rewards.

So, lets dig into the job search process and each of

the "C"s.

Content

Content refers all your job search materials and assets. This is your resume, cover letters, thank you notes, your LinkedIn profile, and social media presence. If you're a creative or technical person, this would include your portfolio or work samples.

Once you have your target clearly defined, and you are ready to take the job search step, it is vital that you have all of these assets in top shape.

Not only do they need to look professional and well crafted, they need to be created with your goal in mind.

As a former Recruiter, I have looked at an unbelievable number of resumes. I don't even want to try to quantify it – it will put me on the couch curled up in the fetal position.

While I found reviewing resumes to be a boring and tedious task, I learned a LOT about what works and what does not help job seekers to connect with their ideal opportunities.

I have seen many resumes and other materials that look nice and are well written. But many of these people complain that they aren't getting interviews.

Upon further inspection, I usually uncover the reason – everything is too general and is not authentic and specific to the individual and the job they truly want.

Don't be afraid to go after what you want. If you've done the work to come up with your desired target, and you've run it through the lens of reality, then you are ready to reach for your realistic but challenging dream.

Or at least the next step on that journey.

When you write your resume and other job search assets with your target boldly stated and supported (this is very important and we cover this in-depth in the Content module of Career Happiness Navigator!), it's time to Connect with others and find out about opportunities.

Connection

Connection is the result of Community, so it pays to do that work in the Career Happiness Discovery process, so you are building your tribe as you're preparing the Map and getting on the road.

Connecting with people who can provide guidance, information, and leads is essential to launching a successful job search. People can and do get great jobs by applying to ads, but that is the *least* strategic way to uncover possibilities.

In the recruiting world, if a Recruiter puts a job ad on an online site and just waits for applicants without doing any proactive sourcing, that is referred to as "posting and praying".

Recruiters who rely on this method are usually not very successful, especially when the economy is good and there are more jobs than qualified people to fill them.

However, even when times are good for job seekers in general, there is always competition for the best opportunities, and especially for those that are uniquely aligned with your talents and desires.

Remember we are narrowing down your targets so that the job with *your name on it* finds you.

If you just "apply and pray" it is also ineffective. It's a passive, lazy way to conduct a job search. I have worked with clients who told me they were applying for a hundred jobs per week without getting call backs.

After working through the Career Happiness programs, they only needed to apply for a handful of selective positions in order to be invited to interview and secure the job offer of their choice.

These clients engaged with people in their Community to help them to better understand the culture of their targeted organizations, or to introduce them to the unpublished job market, or to give them ideas and information about what it's really like to *do* the job they dream of manifesting.

Strong connections help to bypass the gatekeepers and allow you access to information that just can't be gleaned from a job posting online.

Communication

We all know that the purpose of a resume is to get you noticed and invited in for an interview. And if this is news to you, then stay with me and I will make sure you are prepared!

The resume is vital, but every time you communicate in *any way* with a potential job target, you are representing the brand called YOU, and you must be mindful of how you are selling yourself.

The interview is the most important part of the Communication Ticket to Career Happiness Navigation, however there are other ways in which we communicate with potential job leads.

Every time you send an email, have a phone conversation, you send a thank you note, or attach a cover letter you are selling yourself.

Or not.

Here's an important thing to remember - when you are in job search mode, you are always "on."

What I mean is this – every interaction you have with another human being about your job search in any form is an opportunity to sell the product called YOU.

OR to give people reasons *not* to hire you.

I would go so far as to say this includes ALL your interactions.

If you are watching your child play soccer, all the other parents on the sidelines are potential job leads, or at least sources of information. Don't complain to them about your job search or how scared you are or how desperate you are. Don't bitch about your boss or current situation.

If you must do this save it for your partner or mother – but better yet hire a supportive career coach and tell that person. I always tell my clients they can say anything to me, so they don't have to say it to anyone else.

Everyone you encounter can be a lead – your hairdresser might have a friend in a position of influence at your targeted company.

Your neighbor might have just been promoted from the job you covet.

The kid who mows your lawn might have an aunt who runs the whole show at the non-profit you've been blindly applying to for months.

You get the picture.

Even complaining to your partner or mother has negative effects. They probably won't tell someone not to hire you (at least I hope not!), but even the act of speaking negatively tells the Universe that you lack the confidence and skills to achieve your goals. And it makes you feel worse because you are placing attention on negativity, even though you may think it's good to "vent".

It's not.

If you get frustrated, punch a pillow or go for a brisk walk or run.

Listen to music that pumps you up and dance in your living room.

Do whatever you need to do to keep your vibration high and your outlook positive.

Remember that every interaction is an opportunity to shine.

As for the interview, that is also a whole book by itself. If you want more support around interviewing, that module of Career Happiness Navigation is quite robust. It is a crucial skill to master if you want to be a competitive job seeker.

The good news is that many people are unskilled interviewees, and with a little focused work you can become a pro, even if you've struggled in the past or you are holding on to a false belief that you're not good at it.

Anyone can learn to do it and do it well!

Compensation

You may be wondering, "When is Carol going to talk about money? Job satisfaction is great, but I need to earn a good living!"

I hear that loud and clear. Money is something we all need to live, and we need a lot more of it to thrive, provide for our families, and support the causes we believe in.

If you have more money, you have more freedom, flexibility, and choices.

Money mindset is another whole book, and there are many great ones on this topic.

For our purposes in this book, we are going to talk about Compensation and how important it is to negotiate a good deal without appearing greedy, misinformed, or negative.

Again, this is covered in much more depth in the Career Happiness Navigator group coaching program, but here are my thoughts on getting what you're worth.

If a company does not want to pay a fair salary for your skill set, you don't want to work there.

I will go even further and say that if you perceive they are trying to determine out how little they can get away with offering you, you should run the other way.

I know that much popular wisdom in this area advises job seekers that "whoever says a number first loses".

However, in my experience as a Recruiter, this is often untrue.

If you give a Recruiter a number that is lower than what they are expecting you to say, and they suddenly lower the rate because they know you will accept less, that is a foolish and sketchy organization – at best.

When you're buying anything, the cheapest item is not usually the best. And it often breaks or does a poor job. The saying, "you get what you pay for" has a lot of merit.

Companies who seek to lowball candidates may save

some money upfront, but there is no way those organizations are successful long term and will be able to provide you with the opportunities for growth and development you crave.

So, what do you do when asked, "What salary you are looking for?"

Give them a range with the caveat that you aren't sure yet because you need more information about the job and benefits to know if there is a good match and where fair compensation would fall.

If this causes you to get a low offer, then the company is not a good one for you.

Smart, ethical, and growing organizations implement Compensation strategies predicated on hiring the best person for the job and paying them a fair salary without games or tricks.

You should always do your research, so you understand the cost of living, salaries in that industry, and in your field. Being prepared helps the process work much more to your advantage.

Once you receive a job offer, is it appropriate to negotiate?

Yes and no.

If you are asking for more because you truly believe you are worth more, and what you bring to the role commands a better offer, then sure – go ahead and counter-offer.

But be prepared to justify your request. Asking for more because you think this is a negotiating game is foolish and you could end up blowing a dream opportunity.

Like every other part of this process, be strategic. Everyone wants more money – you need to be prepared to back up your desire with facts and calculated persuasion.

If the Recruiter and/or Hiring Manager view you as a demanding jerk, you may blow the offer, or start the job with a bad vibe.

You don't want to make them sorry they hired you before you even begin working.

You will be most successful where you are most appreciated and valued, so choose your Compensation battles wisely.

Or better yet, go where there is no battle.

Culture

Your work environment is almost as important to your job satisfaction as the actual work.

Many people think they hate their chosen field, when they're just in the wrong environment.

Company culture is not easy to assess from the outside. That is why Connection is so important. We can learn a lot from people on the inside.

Research is also essential – we live in a time where people who are both happy and (especially) unhappy like to shout it from the rooftops, or at least in every online forum, review site, and social media platform.

Take a look at what people are saying about what it's like to work at the companies you are targeting. Really think about whether or not you can picture yourself there.

Even something as simple as the physical setting is a consideration.

- Is it urban or suburban?
- What about parking?
- How long is the commute?
- These are the things that make up our day to day existence. That's where we *live*.
- Do you believe in their mission?
- The product or service they sell?

If you are anti-war it doesn't matter how much the defense industry is paying, and if the idea of smoking makes you ill, your ideal career is not with a tobacco manufacturer.

- Do you like a conservative or more casual workplace?
- Do you want to be able to work from home at times?

In my Career Happiness Navigator program, there is a module on Culture that will help you determine what your idea company culture looks like, and help you align your desires with reality.

Many of us have not given much thought to the type of work environments that are conducive to our greatest success and happiness.

One good exercise is to brainstorm this question for each of your past employers:

- What did you want Less or More of in those environments?
- What did you value?
- Why were you proud (or not) to tell people where you worked?
- What drove you crazy?
- What created inconvenience?
- What made you feel so good that you stayed longer than you should have?

This will give you a sketch of what you're seeking in an organization's culture.

Resist the urge to ignore this factor. If you end up mired in the wrong Culture, you will find yourself looking for a job again sooner than you hoped.

Cruise

I know Cruise seems like an odd word to use for this topic, but "Career Management" was too long and clunky.

I like the word Cruise because it indicates ease and smooth sailing. Too often we start a new job and after a brief honeymoon period, things start to fall apart.

Sometimes it happens slowly, as you learn more

about the Culture, or you find out that your Compensation isn't competitive.

Maybe the interviewers did a good sales job of making it seem like things were much better than they appeared.

The boss you were excited to work for in the interview process could suddenly quit, or be transferred or promoted, and you wind up working for the woman from The Devil Wears Prada.

It happens.

Some of these things are out of your control, but the way you react to them *is* under your control.

As is being proactive about your career in the first place.

When you get a new job, you should celebrate. It's a win!

Managing your career doesn't mean you should be continuously in job search mode, or that you shouldn't relax for a minute.

I am all for celebrating and being appreciative of what you've achieved, but don't get complacent again.

Once you do, you might find yourself back in the same position you were in before you did all this hard work. I don't want that for you!

Career management is a lifelong process throughout adulthood. One of the reasons so many people hate their jobs is they do not understand that their careers are something that need attention all the time – not just when they're looking for a promotion, and not only if they get laid off, etc.

Proactively managing your career is a gift to yourself and it goes a long way to prevent a job search from feeling like a life crisis.

Whatever we ignore often ends up managing us.

I'm not suggesting that every adult needs to be enrolled in a career management program for their entire lives (although it would be useful!), but I am encouraging you to consider your career as a living entity that needs your ongoing attention in order to maximize your satisfaction.

Working is a huge part of our adult lives, and we tend to ignore career management in favor of vacation planning, hobbies, and family concerns.

All of those things are also important to becoming and remaining a well-rounded person, but managing your career is just as essential.

If you are miserable in your job and you are doing nothing to fix the problem, it will affect your family negatively.

It will harm your health.

You won't have the time or energy for hobbies, and vacations will be spent dreading the return to work.

Career management is a gift, and an essential part of a healthy life.

Career Cartography

As I mentioned earlier, a pet peeve of mine is when authors of self-help books continuously blather on about their own journeys.

Sure, it can help to illustrate a point, and I hope I have done that well in this guide, but I want you to focus on you, not me.

However, some stories really drive a point home and can help you see how important it is to plan and manage your career.

Unfortunately, I let mine control me for many years, and there were a lot of wasted years where I allowed myself to play the victim, instead of taking charge of my decision. I played small and hid behind relationships and all sorts of self-imposed limiting beliefs to stay stuck. There isn't one thing I have cautioned you about so far that I haven't fallen prey to myself.

So, let's talk about my retail management years, shall we?

Have you ever worked on your feet for over twelve

hours and been called into the girls' fitting room at a popular clothing store at midnight by one of your employees to find that she is buried in a pile of inside out clothing in a ball - in every stall?

In my 20's I was a retail store manager for several different companies, but the longest stint was with a popular children's clothing retailer.

Every back to school season harried moms, bored kids, and annoyed dads would descend upon the store like locusts fighting for the last pair of sale Levi's or package of clearance underwear featuring The Little Mermaid.

Every night the store had to be returned to pristine condition for the next morning's business day, and no one could leave until everything was done.

On this one night, I was particularly exhausted and questioning my life choices big time (like ALL of them), and when Dasi, Daisy, Doozy (I forget her name) called me into the fitting room and showed me that we were nowhere near ready to leave, I just stood in a pile of sparkly tees and fought back the tears.

Then when Vince, my super responsible floor leader, called me back out to the sales floor to show me that there were exactly two shirts left hanging on the girls' wall, I sat down on the floor and freaked the hell out.

The locust parents had bought every damn girls' clothing item on the wall. And it was a HUGE wall. So now we had to fill the wall with merchandise from the back before we could go home.

No one was making enough money or getting anywhere near the satisfaction required for this crap.

Not even close!

But yet there we were, and we finally all busted into hysterical laughter, as deliriously tired people sometimes do when faced with an impossible but required task.

We did our best and I think I called it by three in the morning and decided to come back in the morning. Well, *later* in the morning, as if that was any better.

I went home to take what amounted to a restless *nap*

and decided that I MUST figure out how to get out of this mess.

Unfortunately, because I didn't seek any guidance or direction from anyone who could actually help me, I mired in this misery for years, and then took another step that made it better but still sucked.

And again, and again until it sucked way less and things were okay.

Then I realized I still wanted more.

My Career Happiness Map looked like a monkey drew it with his feet, and then a penguin drove me around in a Big Wheels to find my destination.

But I'm here now, where I longed to be. But it didn't have to take 25 years full of heartache, frustration, and missed opportunities.

I don't want that for you, and I know you don't want to be buried in a pile of inside out clothes at night in a locked store any longer than you must.

So, what did I learn from all of this?

Hmm...let's see - life is short, and monkeys are bad career coaches and penguins are bad drivers, and I wish I had met someone like me (the me of today) who could have helped me with a systematic approach to bettering my career life.

Have monkeys and penguins been leading you astray? If so, I hope you will implement the strategies in this book and reach out for more help and support if you need it.

Now let's talk about the final piece of the Career Happiness Discovery program. It's one you will need to sustain you on the journey, and it's one of the easiest things to lose in the dance of the ups and downs you will likely encounter on the road to Career Happiness.

Confidence

YOU CAN DO IT!

Confidence: a feeling of self-assurance arising from one's own abilities or qualities, the feeling or belief that you can rely on someone or something – Merriam Webster Dictionary

Everyone knows that Confidence is necessary to achieve great things, but why is it so hard to attain and maintain?

Throughout this process, everything we have talked about doing requires Confidence to execute and feeling good about yourself goes a long way towards getting what you want.

As the definition states, Confidence comes from *your own* abilities and qualities.

Notice that it does not say that it comes from praise from others, or a big bank account, or beauty, or the attention of an attractive partner.

Or *any* external source.

The external only comes into play when we look at the second part of the definition – the belief that you can rely on someone or something.

It's important to surround ourselves with the tribe, teachers and tools we can count on.

That's for sure, but they don't give us our personal confidence. They help us to craft a life where we feel good about our own choices and our paths.

No man or woman is an island. We need Community, but first we need to name and embrace our own worth.

You do not have to do everything right to be worthy and confident. Making mistakes and the F word – failure

– are part of a healthy life filled with measured risks and exciting rewards.

The only reason to ever feel bad about yourself is when you knowingly cause another harm.

Remember, the world needs your gifts. And in order to generously share them, you must identify, cultivate, and believe in them.

In this final Ticket to Career Happiness Discovery, we are going to talk about some of the ways that Confidence challenges us and ultimately moves us forward to our ideal lives.

It's OKAY

Here's something I bet you need to hear today:

It's okay if you picked the wrong career. Really, it is, no matter what others may say or how unhappy you are with your choices.

We make choices with the knowledge and emotional intelligence we have at the time. And there are a lot of factors that affect those decisions.

I made some real doozies myself, and if I can turn the car around, so can you.

I've finally done the work and I am the happiest I have ever been. I'm leaping out of bed, and anyone who knows me well knows that's saying something! A am a huge fan of my bed.

Remember my earlier waking time? I would not be making that happen to do something boring or in any way yucky.

- So, what happened to derail your Career Happiness that you need to get over?
- To forgive?
- To let go of to build a more confident, brighter future?
- Maybe you graduated into a bad economy and

didn't see all your options?
- Perhaps you felt pressure from family to choose a certain path?
- Possibly you needed guidance you didn't know how to find?
- Did you allow a partner to control your choices?

Or it's conceivable that you once loved your career choice, but now it no longer fits who you are today.

The list of reasons for a disappointing choice are endless. But they are in the past. Leave them there. The list of solutions is short and simple:

Just make a change. NOW. In this moment. The only one you really have.

I know you may be thinking that I'm full of crap, and that it's not easy to do that, and you may as well just stay where you are. But please don't do that.

There are SOOOO many options for people to pursue their passions, live their dreams, and ask for what they want. First, you must open your mind and heart to the possibility, and then do the work.

Yes, there will be work. But it's FUN work. I promise!

It's work that's all about *you*, and what gets you excited and engaged!

What other choice is there? You can't keep doing what you're doing for the next 10, 20, or 30 years.

Right?

So, give yourself the gift of a better choice, and get the support you need.

Write in your journal to work through this process.

Take the time to really dig into each of the Tickets to Career Happiness Discovery.

Do more reading.

Listen to podcasts.

Expand your world.

My guess is that you've spent more than enough time beating yourself up, regretting the past, or worrying about the future.

So, stop.

Let's stop focusing on what's wrong and talk about what's right.

Celebrate Your Wins

This exercise is short and simple, but in my experience, it is a huge Confidence booster.

If you do something good, write it down.

I think many of us were taught not to brag or "toot our own horns", but when you are seeking Career Happiness you need to toot that baby with all the gusto you can muster.

This is not the time to be shy or to minimize your accomplishments or skills.

If you have never done this, it's a powerful exercise and one that I suggest you frequently revisit.

I had a fantastic boss at one of my former companies who told me that she kept a file in her e-mail of all the messages she received praising her for her work, her results, or her help.

A first I thought that seemed so self-indulgent, but I tried it and it made a huge difference in my Confidence.

It also made my performance self-appraisal much easier to complete. I already had a place where I had stored all my accomplishments and the reasons I deserved a raise and a high-performance rating.

When I am feeling down about myself now, I go to the whiteboard in my office, erase whatever notes are there (they are definitely written somewhere else too so no biggee) and make a list of all the things I've completed, conquered, and moved forward.

Sometimes I just do it for the past week or month.

Or I set a specific milestone – like quarterly or since I launched a particular program and made a change.

And when I am really in need of a self-esteem boost, I go back as far as I can remember and make a very long list of all the challenges I have successfully overcome.

Even if you are a lot younger than me, I would be willing to bet you will have quite an impressive list.

It's nice when other people praise us, and I agree with my former boss, Kelly, that it's powerful and affirming to save those notes of appreciation from others, but in order to achieve a sustained level of Confidence we have to look back at the first part of the definition I shared at the beginning of this section:

a feeling of self-assurance arising from one's own abilities or qualities

Never stop celebrating your wins. If you do this even twice as much as you mourn your losses and beat yourself up for mistakes, your level of success will increase exponentially.

You are a winner! And if you've already achieved so much, you can do it again and again.

So, keep your list where you can see it.

Recite it.

Sleep with it under your pillow.

It's a testament to the real you, and she's the only one you have to worry about.

It's NEVER Too Late!

Have you ever felt like you were too old to make a change? Were you thinking that way when you picked up this book? How about now? Any changes?

I sure hope so.

I know I've felt this way, and I totally understand why women are especially prone to this belief.

For me, as a middle-aged woman I am bombarded with tips of how to wear my makeup, my hair - don't wear dark lipstick, sparkle is a no-no, cut your hair shorter to look more professional, don't go grey or you'll never get a job, etc.

I choose to color my hair because I always wanted to

be blond.

I wear my hair long because that's how I like it.

And I wear bright, dark, and sparkly lipstick all the time, and I don't think it makes me look older. It's a part of who I am, of my self-expression. It makes me look like me.

Why should I tone myself down because I'm older? Are we trying to make the old ladies invisible, so we don't have to look at them or notice them or worry about becoming them?

I don't know about you, but I am inspired by women older than me who are out there doing things, presenting themselves authentically, and not bowing to societal pressures to disappear just because their youth has faded.

But perhaps just as damaging as the attack on our appearance is the attack on our value in the workplace. How often have you heard?

- I am too old to go back to school.
- No one will hire someone at my age.
- I can't start over.
- It's too late.

I want to SCREAM when I hear these statements, most often said about smart, talented, vibrant women who have SO much time to contribute their gifts to the world.

I've even heard women in their mid to late 20's say that they thought it was too late to change careers - "I picked this career, so I have to keep doing it."

WHO MAKES THESE RULES??

- I was 30 before I got out of retail management and on a path to a better career (baby steps but you can do MUCH better!)
- I was 42 when I completed my master's degree.
- I was 46 when I published my first book.

- I was 47 when I married my soulmate.
- I was 49 when I finished my career coaching certification.

Did you wake up today? Then you're good to go!

Why are we letting other people and society feed us this crap? Shouldn't we be fully living our *whole* lives?

If you are still able to work - physically and mentally, and you WANT to contribute your unique gifts to the world, then *no*, it's not too late.

Sometimes it's just fear that holds us back, as we discussed in the Courage section.

Or maybe it's an easy excuse to avoid the problem.

To avoid change.

But change can be AMAZING! Every big change in my life has led me to something SO much better in my career and personal life.

I turned 50 last year, and I went through all of these emotions and fears.

And then I told them all to shut the hell up, and I moved forward with the next steps on my Career Happiness Map.

So, I ask again, did you wake up today?

Then it's not too late, and now is the time to implement and execute the steps of your Career Happiness Map.

The world needs what you have to offer.

If I Can Do It, So Can You!

Why is Confidence the final piece of my Career Happiness Discovery (http://careerhappinessmap.com/work-with-carol/#discovery) process?

Because if you lack Confidence you will allow fear to paralyze you and keep you stuck in a life that you never wanted, and a career that doesn't fit you and your unique gifts and desires.

How will you successfully implement the steps on

your bright, shiny, new Career Happiness Map if you don't believe in yourself?

I know it may seem like I have conquered my problem with Confidence, but I still struggle every day.

It's not something you just fix, like a leaky faucet or a broken nail. It requires constant and vigilant work to maintain the good feelings I have worked so hard to cultivate.

Old habits and limiting beliefs are tenacious in their hold, and it's a daily practice to block their access to my mind and heart.

Since I know you may be feeling like you have a long way to go, and the road may seem daunting, I am going to share a little tidbit of embarrassing, but 100% factual information (you could ask my ex-husband, he'd tell you and we'd just laugh about it now).

Before I tell the story, I want to say that as a child I was very confident. Before puberty and the awkward, angst filled, confusing teen years came along, I was a proud, loud, spitfire of a girl.

I am not sure exactly how I came to lose all Confidence in myself and my own worth, but I suspect it had something to do with boys.

And then men.

I may write a book about that topic someday, but for now the only thing that matters is to know that I started out strong, I slipped far down into the lack of confidence abyss, and clawed my way out.

So here goes.

When I was a young woman (teens to early 20's), I was afraid to order pizza over the phone.

Now when I say I was *afraid,* it's not like I thought the pizza guy was going to come to my house and murder me, or that the pizza would be poisoned, or that the phone was emitting radiation (this was the time period when a cordless phone was the new, modern thing to have).

No, the problem was that I didn't feel confident enough to call a business and ask for... anything.

I felt like the person on the other end of the phone was going to misunderstand me, make me feel dumb, or treat me with disdain, or as an annoyance.

I allowed a pizza guy (it was usually men in my part of the country) to make me feel inadequate.

I have nothing against men who make pizza, and I am sure many of them are very smart and capable humans. But as a smart and capable young woman, I surely had no reason to fear the judgment of the pizza guy.

Plus, he was busy! Those pizzas don't toss themselves into the air. He wasn't schooled in the fine art of phone etiquette. It's not me he was judging negatively – he just wanted to take the order so he could make money and get out of the shop so he could take his girlfriend to the carnival.

Okay, now that sounds like a Bruce Springsteen song, but you know what I mean.

The point is that today I have two very visible businesses - Career Happiness Map (http://careerhappinessmap.com/) Coaching and Fun Feminine Fiction (my fiction author brand).

- I make videos and share them with the world (or at least whoever my social media account shows them to).
- I speak in front of audiences in person.
- I was a trainer in my corporate job.
- I was a Recruiter and had to call about 100 people per day, some who had no interest in hearing from me and didn't mind me knowing that fact.
- I was a Meetup organizer and met new people weekly.
- I did a LOT of online dating, most of which you can read about in my fiction, with names and situations altered to protect the innocent...and guilty.
- I write books and send them out into the world for people to criticize my precious thoughts and stories. And it is one of my greatest sources of joy and

satisfaction!
- I sing karaoke on any stage anywhere. I've sung on stage with a band.

I am no longer afraid of what people think, of being ridiculed, of not being good enough.

So, where did my confidence come from?

- Little wins over time.
- A tenacious spirit.
- A hunger for more.
- Making a PLAN!
- Journaling.
- Self-development work.
- Bringing new people into my circle.
- Eliminating toxic relationships.
- Hard freaking work.
- Continuous learning.
- Passion!

What I would love for you is the knowledge and belief that YOU can do more, be more, have more…and that it isn't as hard as the little scared voice inside you is telling you.

She wants to order the pizza, so when she's ready, I like mushroom on mine. :)

Carol

Carol's Fiction Books

Fun Feminine Fiction

Laughing in Love

Romantic Comedy/Chick Lit

Rom-Com on the Edge Series

Dazed & Divorced (Book 1)
There Are No Men (Book 3)
The Juggling Act (Book 5)
Valentines on the Edge (Short Story Collection)
Let's Hear it From the Boys (A Short Story Collection)

Flirting with Fantasy

Paranormal Rom Com/Chick Lit

Love Pixies Series

Love Pixies (https://www.amazon.com/gp/product/B0738V21WJ/ref=dbs_a_def_rwt_bibl_vppi_i6) (Book 1)

Spooky Matchmakers Series

Nobody Tells Lia Anything (Book 1)
Something Molly Can't See (Book 2)

Join Carol ON THE EDGE

Please go here (https://carolmaloneyscott.com/get-a-free-book/) to become an Edgy Reader and receive a FREE BOOK as my thank you for joining!

The fun doesn't stop with the FREE DOWNLOAD!

As a member of my Edgy Readers Group, you will receive:

- More free books!
- News on upcoming releases!
- Exclusive contests and giveaways!
- Updates on projects and new series in the works!
- Polls asking for your opinion!
- Shenanigans!
- Wiener dog pictures!
- Excerpts!

I can't wait for YOU to join the party!